T0339896

Advance Praise

"Dan's new book *Employee Empowerment: The Prime Component of Sustainable Change Management* is well written and contains a large number of important elements to any/all Human Resource Professionals who understand the value of 'empowerment' and especially those currently working in a manufacturing, distribution or warehousing operation. Human Resource Professionals sincerely interested in pursuing a 'seat in the C-Suite' should read this book and apply its principles. There is nothing more important in 2020 than employee empowerment and change management. The end result is HR becoming recognized as a 'valued contributor rather than an essential business expense.'"

Michael Wilkerson SPHR, CLRP
Director of HR
Advicare

"Dan Bloom has tackled the very elusive aspiration of empowerment of people in organizations and given it a solid framework. He gives the topic of empowerment a holistic review, and makes the business case for why it matters to each employee personally and collectively for effective, and relevant, company cultures. This book gives readers a model and tools to be consistent and successful in fostering empowerment. I highly recommend you get this for your business/HR library."

Steven Browne, SHRM-SCP
VP of Human Resources LaRosa's, Inc.
Author of HR on Purpose!!

"Like all of Dan's books, *Employee Empowerment: The Prime Component of Sustainable Change Management,* is very well written, and I recommend it to all HR professionals and members of company leadership. Dan discusses the importance of employee empowerment and change management in a very interesting manner, which should serve as a guide to all HR employees. I especially enjoyed Dan's section on the various kinds of empowerment in society that exist within most companies. Another section of Dan's book that I truly enjoyed was what Dan referred to as the 'Role of DNA in Life.' Dan's contention is that the basics of genetics can be applied to your business organization and the argument that can be presented is that there is a form of DNA contribution to organizations. Dan explains that as DNA is to life, empowerment guides what our organizations look like and how they behave. I never expected to read about a biological term applying to an HR organization, but Dan has done so very well! Dan ties in the TLS continuum by explaining that Continuous Process Improvement (CPI) consists of four interdependent components and lets the reader know that CPI will not be achieved without the integration of each of the elements. Dan also presents a logic tree, referred to as the Goal Tree, and presents it in the context of the TLS continuum as it applies to empowerment. He creates this logic tree over several different chapters with each chapter adding a new level to it. All I can say is, 'Job well done Dan!'"

Bob Sproull
LSS Master Black Belt and TOC Jonah
Author of nine books on Continuous Improvement

Employee Empowerment

Employee Empowerment
The Prime Component of Sustainable Change Management

Daniel T. Bloom SPHR SSBB

Routledge
Taylor & Francis Group

A PRODUCTIVITY PRESS BOOK

First published 2021
by Routledge
52 Vanderbilt Avenue, New York, NY 10017

and by Routledge
2 Park Square, Milton Park, Abingdon, Oxon, OX14 4RN

Routledge is an imprint of the Taylor & Francis Group, an informa business

© 2021 Daniel Bloom

The right of Daniel Bloom to be identified as author of this work has been asserted by him in accordance with sections 77 and 78 of the Copyright, Designs and Patents Act 1988.

Library of Congress Cataloging-in-Publication Data
Names: Bloom, Daniel, author.
Title: Employee empowerment : the prime component of sustainable change management / Daniel Bloom.
Description: New York : Routledge, 2020. | Includes bibliographical references.
Identifiers: LCCN 2020008910 (print) | LCCN 2020008911 (ebook) | ISBN 9780367002176 (hardback) | ISBN 9780367002169 (paperback) | ISBN 9780429400735 (ebook)
Subjects: LCSH: Employee empowerment. | Industrial management--Employee participation. | Organizational effectiveness.
Classification: LCC HD50.5 .B56 2020 (print) | LCC HD50.5 (ebook) | DDC 658.4/06--dc23
LC record available at https://lccn.loc.gov/2020008910
LC ebook record available at https://lccn.loc.gov/2020008911

ISBN: 978-0-367-00217-6 (hbk)
ISBN: 978-0-367-00216-9 (pbk)
ISBN: 978-0-429-40073-5 (ebk)

Typeset in Garamond
by Deanta Global Publishing Services, Chennai, India

Dedicated to the faculty and students behind the #Never Again movement at Marjory Stoneman Douglas High School who have manifested and lived the TLS Continuum Empowerment Model through both their engagement and empowerment following the mass shooting in their school.

Other Books by Daniel T. Bloom

Achieving HR Excellence through Six Sigma

Field Guide to Achieving HR Excellence through Six Sigma

The Excellent Education System: Using Six Sigma to Transform Schools

Just Get Me There: A Journey through Corporate Relocation

Reality and Perception and Your Company's Workplace Culture: Creating the New Normal for Problem Solving and Change Management

Contents

List of Figures

Foreword

In today's VUCA (Volatility, Uncertainty, Chaos, Ambiguity) world, no company is safe being in neutral and staying the course. Every organization, throughout the world has to evolve and reinvent itself, or it will eventually vanish. With the rapid growth of knowledge and globalization, no company is safe; every firm is in a struggle to survive.

The only resource that is guaranteed to be essential for success is the people of the organization. Whatever happens in an organization, it has to occur via the people.

To motivate your people to give discretionary effort, you need to reach them in a way that captures their imagination for the accomplishment of the company's purpose or vision. It would be best if you consistently treat your people with the behaviors of the values you espouse. It is common to refer to the measurement of the level of employee commitment through engagement surveys. But the current and common approach to building engagement through parties, perks, sleep pods, playrooms and the like is only producing a short-lived positive impact. After the food is gone and the games and parties are over, what is salient in the memory of the employee, is not the artificial "fun" time; rather, they recall how their direct manager treated them. The employee remembers what the leaders said are the correct behaviors for the values versus how the manager acted. The employee recalls the gap between reality and the promise.

What drives the employee to want to help the company move the organization forward is the experience the employee has at work. It is the employee experience (EX) that makes a difference. In Dan's book, he frequently uses the term "human capital asset." The asset is the people. However, unlike the physical assets of an organization, people do not depreciate. I prefer to refer to this as human capital or only people management. The reality is, the more involved your employees are, and the more your people share knowledge, not only do your people grow, but your people build your other assets. Dan points out that the EX is rooted in the company DNA (the company's belief system) and that empowerment is equivalent to human cellular DNA. Like people, the organizations have DNA, and the company's DNA is the values and corresponding behaviors that will define the type of EX that sets the employee experience expectation and, in turn, results in employee engagement. It is your company's EX DNA that is the building block of empowerment.

The power of the nuance of language is also another theme of Dan's approach. Language is especially important when you consider that companies, even in the same industry, and the same geographic location, cannot have the same DNA. As such, no two companies can be the same. Comparing one to the other is like generalizing about the human genome and saying we are all the same. But when you take the DNA test, you find that the smallest of differences could mean a relative match or just another person who was looking at their DNA.

The prevailing traits of the leaders are rooted in the values and behaviors of those who preceded them. To prevail in the organization and maintain the position of leadership, they reinforce correctness by being in charge and hiring and promoting others who have the same or very similar attributes of behavior. Hence, like DNA, it is passed on from one generation of employees to the next generation of employees. When there are those new to the company, who exhibit different, even alternative behaviors, the DNA of the organization kicks into survival gear. Like human DNA, it initially rejects the change. Human DNA eventually mutates because of marriage outside of its insular group or environmental modifications that demand change for survival. It is a slow evolutionary process, much like the change in corporate DNA.

In this book, Dan recognizes the central importance of corporate culture and the power for good, that culture has when based on a set of continuously lived values. He is not trying to say you need to change the culture but rather celebrate your culture and use it as a strong foundation for moving the company to a new understanding of how to execute the business. He makes a strong statement that leaders cannot view their people as depreciating physical assets to be thrown out. Instead of that, human capital is only a positive benefit to the company when it feels respected and trusted. In turn, the employees will feel respect and take on responsibilities and achieve their goals. The employee will be empowered.

From my perspective, there are two signs that the DNA of the company is lived by the leaders. The first is that the leadership is consistent and predictable in how they act, at all times. Consistency in behaviors results in employees having both trust and respect for their direct manager and the C-Suite. Without employees having trust and respect in their leadership, the employee experiences will not be a positive one. If the employee experience is not favorable, then you will not have an active and positive engagement, which in turn means the Continuous Process Improvement (CPI) will not be possible.

Based on this understanding of the central importance of having a reliable company DNA, you will have employees who feel respect and trust. Based on that foundation, you will be able to empower employees to ride the tide of VUCA and find in the turbulence ways of improving, even shifting, the business to new ideas, new products and new heights.

One of the most frequently used strategic drivers of business today is innovation. Dan's book in Chapters 5–8 takes you on a journey presenting how you can use the concepts of Lean and Six Sigma to move your company toward a brighter future while strengthening your company DNA.

Dr. David S. Cohen
DS Cohen & Associates
A member of the #MG100
Toronto, Ontario, Canada

TLS Continuum Empowerment Model Acronyms

CAP Change Acceleration Process
CPI Continuous Process Improvement
CRT Conflict Resolution Tree
DMAIC Define-Measure-Analyze-Improve-Control
DNA Deoxyribonucleic Acid
EMP Empowerment
ENG Engagement
FEE Full Time Equivalent Employee
GE General Electric
HR Human Resources
LSS Lean Six Sigma
MS Management Style
OWN Process Ownership
RCT Randomized Control Trials
ROWE Results Oriented Work Environment
SIPOC Sources-Inputs-Processes-Outputs-Customers (End User)
TMG Cross-Functional Team
TOC Theory of Constraints
TLS Theory of Constraints-Lean-Six Sigma
UN United Nations
VUCA Volatility, Uncertainty, Chaos, Ambiguity

Introduction

Welcome to how to turn your organization into an organization of choice by both your current and future human capital assets and your customers current and future. Welcome to a journey into continuous process improvement through the individuals in your organization. For every time there is a season and for me the time and the season was my immersion into the world of continuous process improvement. It is a world that began over a decade ago with my enrollment into the Applied Technology Department at St Petersburg College to undergo the grueling course of study leading to earning a Certificate as a Six Sigma Black Belt.

This was a journey which totally changed my view of the business world. This new view was centered around the fact that our organizations were whole systems[1] which functioned from a reliance on various processes. It constructed a view that my fellow HR professionals were missing a vital part of their responsibilities to their organizations. A vital part of their responsibilities is to be able to communicate to the other segments of the organization in the language of business. This effort resulted in my ongoing relationship with the editors and staff at CRC Press[2] and Taylor & Francis Group. It is a relationship which at the moment will culminate with eight titles laying out the TLS Continuum process.

The relationship began with the release of *Achieving HR Excellence through Six Sigma*; this book was designed to explain, in a non-engineering manner, to business people and HR professionals in particular, how they can obtain the ability to speak the language of business. The title demonstrated that there was a particular evidence-based metrics that the C-Suite was seeking in order to better understand how the organization was functioning. It demonstrated the importance of the continued improvement process to the sustainability of the organization. I have taken these concepts and extended them to subsequent titles.

1

I followed up the first title with *The Field Guide to Achieving HR Excellence*, which provided the reader with a step-by-step process to bring the concepts into everyday HR departments and bring about lasting improvements. The book contained several case studies of organizations that have implemented the process including one organization that had completed our live training of these concepts with excellent results.

The third book, titled *The Excellent Education System: Using Six Sigma to Transform Schools*, demonstrated that the principles that we discussed earlier can readily be applied in any organization. It is understood that education is a process and so the concepts of the TLS Continuum can easily be applied both in the classroom and the front office.

Having laid out the steps of the TLS Continuum in the first three titles I turned my attention to the discussion of a definitive issue with all continuous process improvement efforts. In any improvement effort there are two very distinct groups at play. The first is the group that sees the problem but believes that the problem is not affecting the bottom line, so it is not of critical importance. The second group takes the opposite view that not only is there a problem, but it is affecting the organization and that it is critical that the organization change in order to remedy the problem.

Picking up on the second view, *Employee Empowerment: The Prime Component of Sustainable Change Management* looks at the second group and introduces the TLS Continuum Empowerment Model.

The discussion of the TLS Continuum Model will lay out how to create an empowered organization. It will do so through the eyes of management, cross-functional teams and the individual human capital assets within your organization. In subsequent chapters I will explain the components of the empowerment model.

In Chapter 1, I will take you through a discussion of what we mean by the term empowerment. I will look at the term in general and specifically in the workplace. In Chapter 2, I will take you back to your science classes in high school and discuss in elementary terms the role of DNA in how we survive as a people. I will explain what would happen if DNA was not present in our lives. In Chapter 3, I will review the belief that empowerment is the business equivalent to the cellular DNA. Our society and our organizations cannot survive without the role and impact of engagement, and engagement is a building block of empowerment. In Chapter 4, I will introduce the TLS Continuum Empowerment Model and its various components. In Chapter 5, I will discuss the relationship between empowerment and engagement. In the remaining three chapters I will break down each of the components in more detail.

This magical word empowerment constructs a different vision of reality. It is a vision of reality which conjures up a wide variety of mental pictures based on moral upbringing and our belief systems created because of them.

Notes

1. A further review of the whole systems concept can be found in the works of Dr. Lawrence Miller at www.lmmiller.com/the-process-of-change/whole-system-architecture/
2. CRC Press released *Achieving HR Excellence through Six Sigma* (2013); *Field Guide to Achieving HR Excellence through Six Sigma* (2016); *The Excellent Education System: Using Six Sigma to Transform Schools* (2017); and *Reality, Perception and Your Company's Workplace Culture: Creating the New Normal for Problem Solving and Change Management* (2019).

Chapter 1

How Do We Define Empowerment?

In her best-selling album *Luck of the Draw*[1], Bonnie Raitt recorded a song titled "Something to Talk About" in which she sang the words "let's give them something to talk about." Look at the media and hear what they are saying. Political activists. Social activists. The question of empowerment of one group or another comes up almost daily. Even classic literature got in the game more than three centuries ago. In 1667, in his book *Paradise Lost*, John Milton wrote "Within Hell Gates til now, thou us impow'rd.[2]" But with all the media chatter, the real question that arises is just what is meant by the term empowerment?

Like beautify, it has many connotations and rests in the eye of the beholder. That does not help us much in the context of this book. There is a wide variety of responses that can be found in the literature. If I Google the term empowerment, Google tells me that there are 265,000,000 hits for the term. If I narrow the search to "workplace and empowerment", the results are reduced to 34,100,000 hits. To ensure we have a common lexicon for empowerment, let me explain the concept.

Let's consider some of the alternatives.

The Merriam-Webster Dictionary[3], one of the oldest and most well-known dictionaries, defines empowerment as being a noun meaning: the act or action of empowering someone or something; the granting of the power, right or authority to perform various acts or duties; the state of being empowered to do something; the power, right or authority to do something. The website Study.com[4] defines employee empowerment as giving employees a certain degree of autonomy and responsibility for decision-making regarding their specific organizational tasks. It allows decisions to be made at the lower levels of an organization where employees have a unique view of the issues and problems facing the organization at a certain level.

If we go the website Roget's InternationalThesaurus.com[5], we find that there are various words that can also be used to define the term empowerment, such as authorize, strengthen, enable, entrust and delegate. Each of these terms represents an action by someone or something leading to a much greater organization or entity. But the words also imply that there is someone outside of yourself granting you authority to do something.

Suggested Activity

> **EXCELLENCE is the result of**
> **CARING more than others think wise;**
> **RISKING more than others think safe;**
> **DREAMING more than others think practical;**
> **EXPECTING more than others find possible.**
>
> ***ANONYMOUS***

Try using Jay Leno's Jaywalking Exercise with your peers at work. Ask them what empowerment means to them both on a personal level and on a work level. As an aside, try asking the management team the same questions. Ask them what the term empowerment means to them. I guarantee that you will receive a wide variety of answers as empowerment lies in the eyes of the beholder. Their responses will be guided by the biases and cultural upbringing that have shaped their growth as human beings. Their responses will also be guided by the biases and cultural upbringing that have shaped their work environment.

Consider your response through two sets of glasses. The first is from a personal stance. The second is to look at the term from an organizational stance. In the previous work, *Achieving HR Excellence through Six Sigma* (2013), we referenced an anonymous quote reportedly on the wall of a building at the US Military Academy at West Point. The words of the quote can be equally applied to the term empowerment. Let me dissect and expand upon the quote.

Empowerment Is the Result of:

CARING More Than Others Think Wise

As an office holder in the C-Suite, you understand that the power of your organization lies within the strengths, knowledge and skills of your human capital assets. In one of our programs available to organizations I pose the question: How do you classify your human capital assets? Are they just a number to you or do they mean something to you in your corporate culture? Do you value your employees as people who can make a meaningful contribution to the success of the organization? Empowerment means that you value the input from the total organization.

RISKING More Than Others Think Safe

Do you recognize who your subject matter experts are in your organization? When a problem arises who do you turn to for resolution? The empowerment effort means that you make a concerted effort to involve the people at the front line as they are the subject matter experts, right to and including the individual contributors. They are the first to see the problems and the first to recognize the solutions to resolve the problems.

DREAMING More Than Others Think Practical

Corporations today rely on an environment based on the idea of VUCA. David Ulrich, in his book *Victory through Organization* (2017), suggests that VUCA defines the intensity and rate of change in an organization[6]. Your organizations need to envision not what is happening today, but what could be tomorrow with every action that you take. Understand that the organization is going to find that circumstances change with each drop of a coin, that there is nothing to guarantee that what works today is going to work in the future. Marshall Goldsmith told us so in his best-selling book, *What Got You Here Won't Get You There*[7], where he observes that the business future is not only surrounded by uncertainty in operations but also financially. The other added factor is the complexity of what we do. Things are not as simple as they used to be. With all the other stresses in the workplace we are also finally confronted with things not being as clear as they used to be. We find ourselves in a world where things don't always mean the same thing to two different audiences. With these factors combined we need to take the time to envision where we believe your organization can be five, ten years out and how the human capital assets are going to play a role in reaching that vision.

EXPECTING More Than Others Find Possible

The time for command and control operations is over. It is time that you understand the impact your human capital assets have on the organization. You need to understand that they are your subject matter experts. They might make decisions that vary from your own but are better for solving the problem and building a stronger organization.

Both the definition for excellence and the definition of empowerment share a common basis. They both require active involvement within the organization. This is the basis of this work. How do we raise the level of human capital involvement within the organization?

You have lived in this global environment and as such your environment has generated certain feelings towards what is empowerment and what is not. Empowerment to an individual living in a democratic society will be much different than to an individual living in, say, a Russia-like environment.

Sharon Grimsley takes the definition a step further by suggesting that empowerment is based in your organizational policies, mission statements and organizational structure[8]. It is also centered on the work environment and the treatment of your human capital assets.

One of the most beneficial tools for use in a continuous process improvement effort is the use of a mind map to visually show your thought process. An example of a mind map can be found in Figure 1.1. As can be seen, empowerment can actually be broken down into nine subtypes of

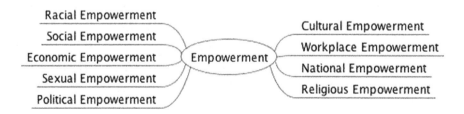

Figure 1.1   Kinds of Empowerment in Society[9].

empowerment. It is also important to understand that while each of the nine can stand on its own, it is our central theme of empowerment that integrates them into a larger concept. Let's look at these empowerment types in more detail.

Racial Empowerment

Throughout history there are examples of civilizations and/or societies who have chosen to marginalize segments of their societies, whether it is African Americans after the Emancipation Proclamation or the ongoing racial divide in general across the world.

There is a worldwide effort on some fronts to reverse this tendency, through racial empowerment programs which represent our first empowerment category in Figure 1.1. Consider these situations: Certain racial backgrounds are relegated to certain professions; certain racial backgrounds are deemed to have less intellect due to their background. What we are referring to here is the instances where particular races of individuals have been accidentally or intentionally left out of functions of the society in which they live and work. We are referring to groups of people who have a history of being considered property rather than a resource for new ideas or innovation. Whether it is African Americans, Latin Americans or people from the Pacific Rim, they have been exposed to conduct which has limited their success in the world as a whole.

Racial empowerment means providing these groups with a new vision of their place in the organization. It talks about programs and services available to these individuals to become vital contributing individuals to both the creation of new ideas and to increasing the introduction of innovations in the way the organization functions. These programs may be financial in nature or they may mean enhanced educational programs. It means elevating their worth in the workplace to provide them greater meaning and purpose. It means empowering them to contribute their ideas and thoughts to the organizational teams.

Social Empowerment

In March of 1969, while serving as an advisor to the Iowa High School Model UN from the Midwest Division of the Council on International

Relations and UN Affairs (CIRUNA)[10], I was asked to deliver the keynote to the 1969 Session. The centerpiece of the presentation was a quote that, while I can't find in its original form after more than half a century, I do remember its essence however. It stated the success of a civilization is not judged by the laws it passes, but rather on how it treats its citizenry. I would contend that the success of a society is judged not by the laws or processes it puts in place but by how it treats its human capital assets.

I began this chapter asking for your thoughts on the definition of empowerment. In my view a society is a model that provides the framework which is united in a common set of standards. United in a common set of goals and objectives. United in a common mission as a whole. United in a vision of where the organization is headed. The Merriam-Webster Dictionary[11] defines society as a companionship or association with one's fellows; friendly or intimate intercourse; in regards to a business environment, a voluntary association of individuals for common ends *especially*; an organized group working together or periodically meeting because of common interests, beliefs or profession; an enduring and cooperating social group whose members have developed organized patterns of relationships through interaction with one another; a community, nation or broad grouping of people having common traditions, institutions and collective activities and interests; a part of a community that is a unit distinguishable by particular aims or standards of living or conduct; a social circle or a group of social circles having a clearly marked identity; a part of the community that sets itself apart as a leisure class and that regards itself as the arbiter of fashion and manners.

The definitions of society reflect some level of empowerment, or the lack thereof, of the individual in society. It reflects the empowerment of the societal human capital assets. These human capital assets are empowered based on their level of engagement. Human capital assets become empowered and thus engaged based on the level to which their contributions are recognized by the organization as a whole.

Earlier we stated that the levels of empowerment in Figure 1.1 were both interdependent and independent. Here is presented the best demonstration of that thought. While each of the empowerment types are discussed below, they would not exist without the involvement of society as a whole.

Later in this book I will suggest this empowerment has a basic key that is the essence of its success.

Economic Empowerment

You can't turn on the nightly news or pick up the daily newspaper without some reference to income inequality. In the current political atmosphere, it is a major subject approached by all persuasions of political thought and dialogue. One of the solutions is to provide avenues for the human capital assets to find greater opportunities to gain wealth and a better life. It comes from empowering the various segments of society to be more successful financially in building their lives. It means providing resources and tools to enable them to grow businesses and communities. It means opening more areas to components of economic gardening[12] or empowering local business in deference to multinational corporations. As the Edward Lowe Foundation states, "Economic Gardening® targets second-stage companies already operating in a community. It helps these existing businesses grow larger by assisting them with strategic issues and providing them with customized research."[13]

Sexual Empowerment

Like the efforts to delineate society based on your race, we also delineate society based on the individual's sexual perspective. Human Rights Watch, #MeToo, Women's March, Equal Pay, Mika Brzezinski's Know Your Value: While not all going in the same direction, they all have the same basis. They all are concentrated on empowering sexual component of society to have more involvement in their own lives. Each is centered on expressing the demands of a particular sex in our society. It is based on the belief that for too long, a sexual component in our society have been treated in a less than fair way. Whether it is how we behave in social situations or in the workplace, career advancement, or the presence of discrimination against a particular sexual orientation which restrict the empowerment of certain members of society. It also is not just female in nature. Not too long ago a recruiter posted on social media that she would never schedule an interview with someone with gray hair.

An empowered organization changes the nature of the organization to consider each of these points of view and realize that gender does not demonstrate the value to the organization. Further it empowers these groups to get out of a limited view of what their role is in our modern society. Sexual orientation or preference does not limit you to certain professions or careers. There are many examples from NASA to C-Suite where sexes differing from the norm have demonstrated their value.

Political Empowerment

Read or listen to the news of late and there is a great deal of discussion around the efforts of some interests to suppress the right to vote for certain groups. On the flip side of the coin are organizations like Andrew Gillum's Bring it Home, Cecile Richards' Supermajority, Rev. Al Sharpton's National Action Network, Stacey Abrams' New Georgia Project and David Hogg's Make Lives Matter. Each has a different audience. Some are local while others are national in scope. What they do have in common is the goal to get our human capital assets involved in the politics of this country, getting them registered to vote, getting them involved in an active fashion with the political discourse on topics ranging from reproductive rights to criminal justice reform. We saw this carried out during the Women's March on Washington and the Black Lives Matter demonstrations worldwide. It means empowering the citizenry to take action on the issues that matter to them instead of sitting on the couch hoping that the change will come.

Cultural Empowerment

A subset of the societal empowerment picture is the ability for individual segments of that society to feel empowered enough to have a dual vision of the world they live in. On one side is the societal view we discussed earlier, and on the other side is their cultural aspects. We see this in the existence of enclaves around the United States, where these cultural units survive unto themselves. Consider Koreatown in Los Angeles, the Pico Boulevard section of Beverly Hills for the ultra-religious Jews, Chinatown in Boston and New York City, Little Italy in Chicago, New York City and San Francisco. In each of these areas the residents are American but they also maintain the elements of their native culture from retail stores, to churches, to language and customs and events.

National Empowerment

There is a big push worldwide for a nationalist view of the world. The interests of the nation in which you reside take priority over the interests of other nations in the world. This empowerment looks at the role we play, how we conduct trade, how we deal with the politics of other nations and how we treat other nationalities. Do we operate from a point of strength or do we single out those populations who don't look like we do?

Religious Empowerment

The second to last empowerment type in Figure 1.1 is that of religious empowerment. This United States of America was founded on the principle of religious freedom as described in the Declaration of Independence and the Constitution.

Those rights lay out a roadmap whereby there is no one single set of religious practices in the country. It further lays out an environment where human capital assets are encouraged to practice those beliefs. The empowerment comes from the ability to practice those beliefs in public view without the fear of retribution for doing so. I recognize in the political climate we are in we do not always reach that plateau but the democratic model we are in allows us to do so.

Workplace Empowerment

The final empowerment type in Figure 1.1 is that of the workplace empowerment, which is the basis of this book. In the coming chapters I will take you through a model of empowerment which emphasizes the role that human capital assets play in that empowerment. I will present the argument that this form of empowerment and its components are the roadmap to the success of your organization.

Before we continue let me discuss one more aspect of this view. I could have written a full book on the discussion of each of the empowerment types, but I won't do so. I am more concerned with the fact that the empowered organization is the primary key to sustained continuous process improvement through the TLS Continuum.

Notes

1. Raitt, Bonnie. "Something to Talk About", *Luck of the Draw*, 1991: Capitol Records.
2. As presented on Empower House's website. https://empowerhouseonline.com/empowerment-the-definition/
3. Merriam-Webster's Dictionary. Definition of Excellence. www.merriam-webster.com/dictionary/empowerment
4. Study.com. Definition of Employment Empowerment. https://study.com/academy/lesson/employee-empowerment-definition-advantages-disadvantages.html
5. www.thesaurus.com/browse/empowered
6. Ulrich, David. *Victory through Organization*. New York, NY: McGraw-Hill, 2017. Pages 10–11.
7. Goldsmith, Marshall. *What Got You Here Won't Get You There*. New York, NY: Marchette Press, 2007.
8. Taken from Sharon Grimsley's online course found at https://study.com/academy/lesson/employee-empowerment-definition-advantages-disadvantages.html
9. Types of Empowerment. https://slideplayer.com/slide/10969244/
10. CIRUNA or the Council on International Relations and UN Affairs was the collegiate affiliate of the United Nations Association of the United States of America.
11. Merriam-Webster's Dictionary. Definition of Society. www.merriam-webster.com/dictionary/society
12. Created by the Edward Lowe Foundation and pushed by the former Economic Development Director of the city of Littleton, CO Chris Gibbons. It called for the economic development in an area to be concentrated on the development of the local businesses rather than multinational organizations. www.national-centereg.org/
13. Definition taken from the Edward Lowe Foundation website. https://edwardlowe.org/entrepreneurship-programs/economic-gardening/#1524834726242-9d3a191b-60a6

Chapter 2

The Role of DNA in Life

Empowerment is a major area of discussion in the HR arena and in the corporate world. Many a human resources professional has tried to explain empowerment. There are numerous books on this word. Since there is no universally accepted definition within the world of business let me add to the discussion by linking the concept of empowerment to genetics. Many of you may be asking why are we discussing genetics in a business book? The purpose of the discussion here is to look at the way deoxyribonucleic acid

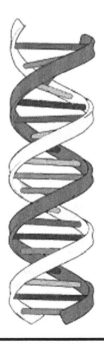

Figure 2.1   DNA Double Helix.

plays a role in determining the characteristics of who we are. My contention is that the basics of genetics can be applied to your business organization. The concept can be presented that there is a form of DNA contribution
to our organizations. If you go back to your high school biology classes,
approximately three and half weeks are spent on the topic. As we will see
below and in the next chapter, once you have a feel for the basics of genetic
models you can extrapolate them into a business model.

The Genetic Timeline[1]

The interest in the basis of our characteristics can be traced back to the
early 1800s. Friedrich Miescher (1844–1895) was involved in the study of
tissue makeup. Part of this study was to identify the molecules that make
up cells. Miescher's area of study was the composition of white blood cells.
What he found was that when you introduced additional molecules or
substances into the cell it changed its nature. He essentially discovered the
importance of nucleic acid in cells.

In 1871 Miescher published his findings in which he stated the distribution of hydrogen, oxygen, nitrogen and phosphorous, with a cellular unique
ratio of phosphorus to nitrogen.

Five years earlier Gregor Johann Mendel (1822–1884), who is considered
the Father of Modern Genetics, discovered the fundamental laws of inheritance. He divided the process into three distinct laws.

The first law or the Law of Segregation determined that each trait is
defined by a gene pair. As we will see in the next chapter, we will observe
the same pattern in the business world. Mendel's second law was the Law of
Independent Assortment. He determined that the genes of different traits are
served separately from the others so that the two genes are not dependent
on another. His final law was the Law of Dominance. It took until 1900 for
the full impact of these laws to be appreciated.

In 1902, Walter Sutton (1877–1916) published the results of genetic
research which showed that each chromosome is different and that the process of meiosis reduces the total number of chromosomes in the long run.

In 1944, Erwin Chargaff (1905–2002) began to study DNA and looked at
the way traits are carried from one organism to another. He was the one
who determined that the DNA molecule could be split down the middle,
each half gathering the same traits as the other half. Chargaff developed the
Chargaff rules of inheritance. The first rule stated that in any species the

ratio of adenine and thymine is 1:1. However the ratio of adenine to guanine will vary from species to species. In the long run the amount of guanine will be equal to the amount of cytosine and the amount of adenine will be equal to thymine. In the next chapter, Chargaff's rules of inheritance are applied to the business world.

In 1881 a German biochemist, Albrecht Kossel, discovered the four building blocks of DNA by identifying the four nucleic bases from which DNA (deoxyribonucleic acid) functions. These four nucleic bases are named adenine, cytosine, guanine, and thymine.

In the 1950s, James Watson and Francis Crick developed the double helix as seen in Figure 2.1. In the Watson and Crick model of DNA, the DNA appears as a double-stranded antiparallel, right-handed helix. The outside strand represents the phosphate backbones. The inside helix strand is the nitrogenous pairs that hold the DNA strands together. These two strands as mentioned above are antiparallel which means they run in different directions.

The basis of the base pairs is the notion that if you have adenine it must be matched with thymine on the opposite strand and likewise guanine must be matched with cytosine on the opposite strand.

While our study of genetics is in no way designed to be a concise study of genetics as you would get in a high school biology class, it is designed to lay the groundwork for the next chapter as we apply these concepts to the business world.

Note

1. The information in the Genetics Timeline is sourced from information on the DNA From the Beginning website. www.dnaftb.org

Chapter 3

The Role of DNA in Business

The discovery of the double helix (Figure 3.1) and of DNA in particular was a crowning event in our understanding of the factors that dictate how our image appears and thinks. The value of our discussion regarding empowerment is that like DNA it was and is a crowning event in regard to how our organizations operate in the VUCA world we live and survive in every day. In this chapter, the discussion turns to the idea that empowerment plays the same role as DNA. Rather than from a biological viewpoint, the view is from

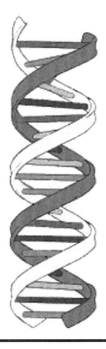

Figure 3.1   DNA Double Helix.

the business world. In the previous chapter, I presented a CliffsNotes version of the concepts behind genetics. Some of you may still be asking: Where is the correlation? The purpose of Chapter 3 is to explain that correlation.

Mendel's laws of inheritance provided the basis for what we look like. It provides the basis for the way we are alike with our relatives and why we are different. He laid these ideas out in his three laws of inheritance. My belief is that the three laws can be directly applied to the question of empowerment in organizations. Like life itself, the business world has its own version of DNA and this is called empowerment. As DNA is to life, empowerment guides what our organizations look like and how they behave. Let's look at how this applies to the business world.

The Law of Segregation

Mendel discovered that each trait is defined by a gene pair. Likewise, your organization is defined by a unique pair of business "nucleic acids." What is important is that they are present in every organization; the difference is in what amount they are present or in what form they are present.

In the DMAIC (Define-Measure-Analyze-Improve-Control) process, one of the tools in the DMAIC toolbox is that of benchmarking. Lynne Hambleton, in her *Treasure Chest of Six Sigma Growth Methods, Tools, and Best Practices*[1], defines benchmarking as comparing your organization with an external organization. As human resource professionals, we have all done it. We have a problem, so we go out into the marketplace and see what others are doing to resolve the same issue. We look at organizations from the same industry clusters. We look at organizations of the same size, both financially and by the number of full-time employees (FTE). The reported idea behind the concept is to identify potential solutions to your internal problem. However good benchmarking has been for organizations, it has its fallacies. The data retrieved from outside organizations is only good for those organizations and those situations. It may not apply to your situation. It may assist with another part of the TLS Continuum Empowerment Model, which will be explained in later chapters in this book.

Every organization is unique unto itself. It has its own cultural norms. It has its own management style. It has its own values. It has its own mission statement. It has its own goals. It has its own work environment. Even though your benchmarking target is in the same industry, and is the same size, it may not have matching criteria. Mendel's Law of Segregation is applied to the business world due to these factors. Your organization and every organization have these components that come to a head when you have a problem that needs resolution. These components and the degree to which they are applied demonstrate how the organization operates.

The Law of Independent Assortment

Mendel stated that genes for different traits are sorted separately from one another so that the inheritance of one trait is not dependent on the inheritance of another. This is found in the business world, for example, while a mission statement is a mission statement, it may not be the mission statement for your organization. Your goals may not be the same as your competitor's. Therefore, the various components of the organizational structure will be applied separately. They will be applied to your organization and only to your environment.

The Law of Dominance

Mendel's Law of Dominance states that one trait will conceal the presence of another trait for the same characteristic. Consider your organization's management style. Some managers still find themselves embedded in the command and control work environment. We have all experienced this type. They are the individuals who tell their employees "this is what I want and this is when and how I want it."

If you bring in a new manager who has worked in a cross-functional team environment where decisions are made by consensus, then it is possible that in order to function in your organization the new manager will have to comply with the command and control management style. We see this in the way our human capital assets are treated. We find this in the level of engagement within our organizations.

Empowerment in your organization can be considered from two different but interdependent views which can be demonstrated from two formulas as can be seen below.

Continuous Process Improvement

One prevailing premise of the LSS or DMAIC perspectives is that there is always a better way. There is no such thing as the perfect process. There is no such thing as the perfect organization. It is this search for the "better way" that we become involved in with continuous process improvement. It means as we work our way through a given process, we are looking for obstacles which hinder the flow of materials and data through the supply chain.

We can construct a formula as shown below to explore the necessary ingredients to achieve the CPI within your organization.

$$\textbf{CPI} = \textbf{MS} \times \textbf{EMP} \times \textbf{ENG} \times \textbf{TMG}$$

Continuous Process Improvement consists of four interdependent components. CPI will not be achieved without the integration of each of the elements. Miss any one of the four elements and continuous process improvement fails to happen. The missing element serves as the anon of continuous process improvement efforts.

The first of these elements is the organizational Management Style (MS). The organization's management style refers to how the C-Suite and middle management office holders treat the other human capital assets of the organization. Reviewing the business knowledge base, we find that most scholars divide the field into two very different types of management styles. The first is that of the command and control manager. We have all had them. Does this sound familiar?

"I need this done and need it done now."
"Never mind what you learned in that seminar, do it this way."

In one of my program options we offer a program titled "Who Am I?: The Role of Human Capital Assets in the Global Workplace." The program begins with asking the participants how they categorize their human capital assets. If the responses say they are expenses, or that they are a ledger issue, they are command and control advocates. Human capital assets are considered a necessary fact of doing business but are not really an integral part of the organization. If one leaves, that is okay, we will just find a replacement.

The second element in the formula is Empowerment (EMP). The empowered organization realizes that your human capital assets are non-owned leased corporate assets. They play a vital role in your organization and must be respected for that role. In today's marketplace, they can take their skills anywhere at any time. In the later chapters and in the next formula we will look at this point in more depth.

The third element in the formula is that of Engagement (ENG). In order to create an empowered organization involved in continuous process improvement, we need to have an engaged workforce and a customer base. Engagement looks at whether your human capital assets' sole purpose for coming to work is collect that paycheck.

CPI requires the intercession of problem-solving teams. So, the final element is that of *Teamwork* (TMG). As we will see, the key is the type of team that is involved. Is it a closed process where groupthink rules or are the teams open to looking at alternatives? Does it involve external resources to reach an appropriate resolution of the problem?

If we review the above formula, each of the elements could most likely create its own mind map of the components that make up the broader factor. However, since we are primarily concerned with the concept of empowerment, let's consider that more in detail.

Empowerment

Like the discussion of Continuous Process Improvement above, we can create the same interdependent formula for the area of empowerment. Unlike its sister formula above, this one consists of only three factors.

$$\textbf{Empowerment}\left(\textbf{EMP=ENG}\times\textbf{TMG}\times\textbf{OWN}\right)$$

As in CPI the first element is that of Engagement. It considers the active role that the various stakeholders play in the organizational processes. It is both the external and internal stakeholders. It is worth our time to stop for a moment and define what we mean by stakeholders.

In 1984, Dr. Edward Freeman[2] suggested that stakeholders are any entity that is either affected or can affect the business processes. Dr. Freeman's concept suggests that we take a broader view of the organization to take into consideration how our actions and processes affect the entire global perspective of the outputs of our organizations.

Engagement is a critical factor in both the CPI and Empowerment arenas due to its descriptions of the roles of each contributor to the end result. Engage for Success states that engagement is a

> workplace approach resulting in the right conditions for all members of an organization to give of their best each day, committed to their organization's goals and values, motivated to contribute to organizational success, with an enhanced sense of their own well-being.[3]

According to the 2018 Engagement Research from Gallup[4] about half of your employees are not engaged, meaning your organization is not being as effective in resolving problems as it needs to be to reach continuous process improvement on a meaningful level.

The second element of the empowerment formula is that of Teamwork (TMG). In the chapter on cross-functional teams we will delve more deeply into this issue. But at this juncture it is important that the concept of teamwork be construed as broadly as possible. The ideal team is comprised of both internal and external stakeholders. It needs to express diversity in regard to skills, backgrounds and thoughts as much as possible.

The final element of the Empowerment formula is that of Ownership (OWN). If I see something wrong with a process, what is the path to correct it? Dictionary.com tells us that one of the definitions for ownership is legal right of possession. In our view this means we need to address who has control over the processes. From this frame of reference then, when a problem is uncovered does the responsibility for resolving the issue reside only with the C- Suite or does it permit the real SMEs in the company to make the correction? We will cover this question of process ownership in Chapter 8.

With the work of some of the pioneers of genetics the discovery was made that DNA in our bodies was constructed from nucleotides in the form of adenine, thymine, guanine and cytosine. While they don't follow the Chargaff rule, the "nucleotides of the business world are the elements of the formulas we discussed above." As we will see later in Chapter 8, the combination of the elements determines what our organizations look like.

The question then before us is: How do you know if you are an empowered organization? We can answer that question by looking at the work of Patricia Lotich. She authored an article titled "13 Characteristics of an Employee Empowered Culture"[5]. In this article Patricia Lotich sets out, as mentioned, 13 characteristics of empowered cultures. Let's review the list from the point of view of our material in this book.

Characteristic #1: Management Committed to Supporting an Empowered Culture

The organization functions based on the view from the top. If management plays at the game of empowerment then, as we will see in Chapter 5, the effort to create organizational empowerment will fail. What do we mean by playing the game of empowerment? The managers who function from the command and control perspective are playing the game of empowerment.

There can be no real continuous process improvement if management stands in its way. Consider the response from a recent Road to Business Excellence class. Part of that program is for attendees to bring a problem from work and create a project to resolve that problem. In the evaluation form submitted, the participant stated that the least valuable part of the seminar was the final project because management would never let them solve the problem the way the project was presented.

Characteristic #2: Empowerment Centered on the Voice of the Customer

There are two perspectives of the customer that an organization can have. The first is that they are, in essence, a nuisance. They are there to purchase your products and you know better than they what their needs are. The other view is that they can be a true partner to your organization. *Harvard Business Review* in the September 2016 issue of their magazine ran an article[6] titled "Know Your Customers 'Jobs to Be Done'." It stresses that you need to understand your customers from the inside out.

The central premise of LSS, DMAIC and the TLS Continuum is that the purpose of each of them is to meet the voice of the customer. They tell us what is bothering them. They tell us what they need to be successful. Jack Welsh, in his presentation to a GE stockholders meeting, stated that the best Six Sigma projects begin not inside the business but outside it, focused on answering the questions—how can we make the customer more competitive? What is critical to the customer's success? … One thing we have discovered with certainty is that anything we do that makes the customer more successful inevitably results in financial return to us.

Characteristic #3: Management Releases Some Level of Control

I previously made reference to the command and control views of some managers. Empowerment requires that management must willingly release some of that control. In this VUCA era we are in, the success of our organizations is dependent on taking advantage of all the resources available. Jeremy Heimans and Henry Timms in their book *New Power* talk about the new way our human capital assets operate in resolving problems which do not lend themselves to being ruled by an iron fist. Problem solvers need to be free to go where they need to get results. This release of control can also be found in the Results Only Work Environment espoused by Cali Ressler, who suggests that work should be based on results, not how we get there.

Characteristic #4: Employees Retrained

CPI and the VUCA environment both require changes to our organizations. We need to see the problems, feel the problems and create a new normal for the organization, which more often than not is a new corporate culture. This leaves you with two directions to take the organization. The first is those who can't do the job are forced out; the second is to take the time to provide them with the new skills through specific training programs. The goal is to provide them with the tools to meet the new demands of the organization and its stakeholders.

Characteristic #5: Free Flow of Information and Data through the Organization

Empowerment means that everyone from the maintenance department to the C-Suite needs to understand how the organization functions. This only comes from the free flow of information and data on performance levels. If asked I should be able to explain to someone how and why a particular process is either working or not working and what solutions would correct the errors.

Characteristic #6: Managerial Trust

Ever hear the statement: Why should we train them because once we do, they will leave? Ever hear the statement: Those employees are lazy, and they come to work only for that paycheck? An empowered organization requires management to trust the human capital assets to do the right thing. Not the right thing in their eyes but in the eyes of the people directly affected by their decisions. It means that management understands that this is not the age of the old-fashioned workplace and they need to refocus their efforts to reflect this change.

Characteristic #7: Autonomy Comes with Expectations and Boundaries

In no way are we suggesting that you turn your organization into a free-for-all. That is not good for your customers, your human capital assets or the organization as a whole. The ROWE method says that if you have a project due, the important factor is that you have it done when the project milestone is reached. Whether we are talking about the GE Workout or CAP process, they both come with boundaries of some sort. They both come with the expectation that the work will be completed by a certain time period.

Characteristic #8: Provision of Coaches

With the expectations and boundaries there will inevitably be human capital assets who do not meet those boundaries and expectations. The empowered organization has in place the resources to provide those individuals with assistance to reach the acceptable levels of performance. These resources include a robust coaching program. Jeffrey Liker in his books about the Toyota Production System discusses how the manager's role includes the coaching of employees who do not meet the required production levels. The coaching may mean coaching them out of the organization if they can't reach those levels.

Characteristic #9: Provision of Advanced Training and Coaching

Some of the changes are going to require advanced skills. The organization must be ready to provide advanced skill training and additional coaching for those who need it.

Characteristic #10: Compensation and Benefits Aligned with Organizational Strategies

A large question in the marketplace today is the question of compensation equity. Are we paying one population less for the same job and skills and why? The empowered organization will adjust the compensation and benefits to reflect interorganizational equity but also ensure that the compensation levels are equivalent to the outside marketplace. While compensation and benefits are not the sole reason one accepts a position, they still play an important role in the decision. It does not help your situation when your human capital assets can leave for higher pay in another organization.

Characteristic #11: Job Matching

The empowered organization conducts extensive job analysis to ensure that the skills of your employees are correctly matched with the jobs they are in. This does not mean that you construct mismatched requirements, for example, requiring a higher degree when the job can still be performed without it. The ultimate goal is that you want the right person in the right job in the right place at the right time. The goal is to, yes, have coaching in place but at minimal levels. Therefore, everyone must be in the position that best represents their skill sets.

Characteristic #12: Employees Have the Right Tools to Complete Their Responsibilities

It is equally critical that once you have the correct process in place, that the empowered human capital assets have at their disposal the right tools to complete that process. It serves no one when your customer needs your product or service and they can't get it because you can't deliver due to obstacles in the way.

Characteristic #13: Implementation Plan Is in Place

Empowerment is worthless if we do not have a plan to reach that goal. Part of the TLS Continuum is to change the organization to a new normal. There has to be in place a clear set of steps to that. The implementation must encompass the specific steps, goals and outcomes that are expected through the change process.

The implementation plan must include who is responsible for what part of the plan, when it must be completed and what the next step is, and then in the following step, who gets the handoff and what must they do at that point. It must include the milestones going forward.

The Empowerment DNA of Business

While DNA is the basis of animal genetics, empowerment is the equivalent basis for business genetics. It is the embodiment of who we are as an organization. The TLS Continuum provides us with a roadmap to reach that empowerment. In the following chapters we will look at the TLS Continuum as a whole and then the TLS Continuum Empowerment Model in specifics. In Chapter 5 we will look at the management contribution. In Chapter 6 we will look at the contribution of cross-functional teams and, finally, in Chapter 7 we will look at the role of the individual in empowerment efforts.

Notes

1. Hambleton, Lynne. *Treasure Chest of Six Sigma Growth Methods, Tools, and Best Practices*. New York, NY: Prentice Hall, 2008. Page 160.
2. Dr. Edward Freeman created the Stakeholder Theory which is a view of capitalism that stresses the interconnected relationships between a business and its customers, suppliers, employees, investors, communities and others who have a stake in the organization. The theory argues that a firm should create value for all stakeholders, not just shareholders. http://stakeholdertheory.org/about/
3. Engage for Success. https://engageforsuccess.org/what-is-employee-engagement
4. https://news.gallup.com/poll/241649/employee-engagement-rise.aspx
5. Lotich, Patricia. "13 Characteristics of an Employee Empowered Culture." https://thethrivingsmallbusiness.com/empowerment-a-leadership-competency
6. Christensen, Clayton et al. "Know Your Customers 'Jobs to Be Done'." *Harvard Business Review*: September 2016. https://hbr.org/2016/09/know-your-customers-jobs-to-be-done

Chapter 4

The TLS Continuum Empowerment Model

What Is the TLS Continuum?

Several times in previous pages of this book we talked about the TLS Continuum. For those of you who have read any of my earlier books, you will have seen and read the explanation of just what it is. For those who have just picked up this book and are not sure what the TLS Continuum is, let us look at a brief explanation of the theory and the process.

The letters TLS stand for the three components of the continuum. The letter **T** stands for the Theory of Constraints. Created by Dr. Eliyahu Goldratt in his book *The Goal*, it is a critical thinking based system for determining where the obstacles lie within your organization. Through the use of various tools, it asks you to determine where the obstacles are in the process. The purpose of the TOC involvement in the continuum is to determine what needs to be changed, how to change it and how do we accomplish the change. TOC or Theory of Constraints operates at the level of the chain looking for the weakest link. It is in essence the hypothesis of the problem-solving method overall.

The letter **L** stands for Lean. Most organizations are familiar with the concept of Lean. It is centered around removing waste from the organizational processes so that the customer receives their orders faster. Understand that faster may not mean cheaper or better quality, it means only that we expedite the process.

The final letter is **S** and it represents the concepts of Six Sigma. The primary goal here is to remove variation from the processes.

If we combine the three letters of the acronym, what we find is that the TLS Continuum is organized around a process in itself. We use the Theory of Constraints to locate and identify the obstacles within the system. What is holding up the process? Where is the weakest link in the process? Bob Sproull has provided the perfect view of this action in his piping diagram as shown below. From the diagram you can clearly see that the weakest link is the point where the flow is narrowed at Point E. With the introduction of TOC, the system asks you to elevate the obstacles and determine how to remove them (Figure 4.1).

We use Lean to do what it is meant to do and that is to remove the obstacles. We have identified the obstacle and determined through the critical thinking tools how to remove that obstacle and then use the Lean tools to actually remove the waste.

Finally, the system utilizes the Six Sigma tools to create the standard of work and remove any variation from the process. When we do this, we have completed the improvement process by creating a progressive system for resolving the problems that occur within many organizations. It is an evidence-based effort to identify, remove and improve the system so the problem does not reoccur.

How does this apply to the workplace? The TLS Continuum provides you with a roadmap to guide you through the improvement process. When we

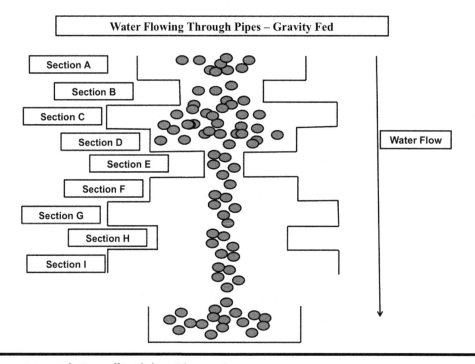

Figure 4.1 Bob Sproull's Piping Diagram[1].

recognize that the improvement process is tackling a world system as proposed by Dr. Lawrence Miller[2], then we understand that the TLS Continuum is a vital tool in resolving those world system problems and system obstacles. It is a dynamic system designed to provide you with new insight into how your organization operates and processes flow. The organization is not concerned with whether you are talking about a process that produces something or a process that produces a need. The steps of the process can be clearly delineated as shown below.

The TLS Continuum Process

The TLS Continuum Process consists of a series of logical steps to bring improvement to the process involved. Each of these steps builds on the previous step to develop a fully concise effort to resolve the problem at hand.

Step 1: Determine Your Goal

What is your company's goal? Let me ask that again: What is your company's goal? Eliyahu Goldratt, in *The Goal*, says that every organization's goal is to make money. Tony Alessandra, in *The Platinum Rule*, says the goal is to acquire and maintain customers. Whatever the goal is, you need to clearly delineate it.

Part of the process to determine the goal is to change the organizational view of the world. We no longer calculate things based on cost. Our view must transform to a look at throughput. Costs are not allocated to a particular product or service; rather they are allotted over the entire process. We do this through the implementation of throughput accounting. The formula for calculating the new view is that throughput is the rate of new sales dollars. In other words, it is the total sales dollars minus the total variable costs to produce the end product.

$$\textbf{Net Profit} = \textbf{Throughput} - \textbf{Operating Expense}$$

$$\textbf{Return on Investment} = \left(\textbf{Throughput} - \textbf{Operating Expense}\right)/\textbf{Investment}$$

In order to determine the ROI or net profit we subtract those product costs from the amount of sales. Inventory or investment costs are the funds you have put into machinery and materials to produce your products. The remaining factor is the organization's operating expenses. This provides us with a view of monies traveling through the organization.

With the goal in mind, we turn our attention toward where we need to get. William Dettmer[3] and Bob Sproull[4] suggest the use of a Goal Tree. An example of one appears on page 34.

The Goal Tree begins with your goal. What is it you are trying to achieve? It then poses the question: In order to reach this goal, your organization MUST have what? What is the critical success factor which tells you that you have reached the goal?

With the critical success factors in place the next level down in the tree is to ask: In order to obtain the critical success factors what must be in place to reach the goal? What changes in your process will be required to get the new factors in place? In the example in the chart that follows, that organization determined that they wanted to maximize throughput. In order to secure that maximized throughput they needed to maximize incoming sales dollars while controlling costs. As we did with this level, the next level down asks you to determine what you need to, for example, maximize revenue. The example tree shows that the way you do that is to have satisfied customers.

Finally, at the bottom of the tree you ask again what is needed for you to have satisfied customers. In the example on the next page it suggests that you need to have a high-quality product. This would bring us back to the customer side of the equation and causes us to question whether there is something about your product which is not meeting the needs of your customers.

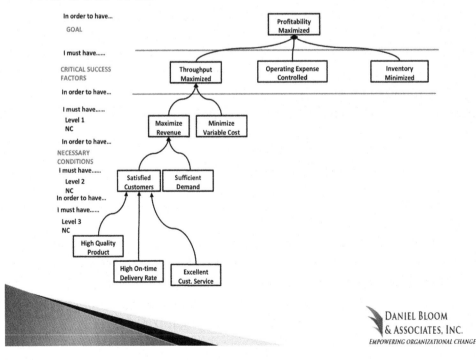

The Goal Tree

Step 2: Define the Boundaries

With the goal and its prerequisite in place, we can turn to trying to resolve the issue at hand. The process begins with two critical parts to the TLS Continuum process.

The first task is the development of a project charter. A project charter presents several key elements for our consideration. The underlying tenant of the charter is that we see and feel the needs of our customers. With the charter in place we can construct what the solution seeking process is going to appear like. The project charter consists of 11 sections which enables the organization to walk through the improvement process and gain an understanding of where the organization is and where it expects to be at the end of the problem-solving effort. The first section asks for identification of the problem, presented in a short sentence as to what the problem (goal) is. The following section asks you to identify the organization for whom the solution seeking effort is being undertaken.

Every solution seeking effort should include someone who serves as the gatekeeper, if you will, between the project and management of the two firms involved. They are responsible for paving the way for the cross-functional team to perform the actions they need to accomplish the goal they have established.

The second task is the development of the cross-functional team. The process of constructing a team will be discussed at length in Chapter 6.

Starting with a macro view your cross-functional team should include a representative of all the stakeholders who play a part in the process. It means identifying who has an investment in the solution to the problem. Once the team is in place and the milestones or deliverables have been identified, there is still one other crucial decision to be made. With the help of the project sponsor and the project champion, you need to determine the chain of command for process changes. Does the team have the power to make the changes on its own initiative? Does the cross-functional team have the authority of management to enter into the solution seeking effort? Remember the purpose of your change effort is to see the problem, feel the problem and change the organization to create a new normal. Is there organizational buy-in to create that new normal business model? Without that tacit approval you can be looking for solutions every day and still not respond to the customer's voice about your processes.

Step 3: Identify the System Constraint or Obstacle

Using the critical thinking tools of the TLS Continuum, the next step is to define the problem. What does the system tell you the current state looks like as well as what the future state will look like after the solutions sought are implemented? What are the characteristics of those state components? What does the system look like? From there we can begin to commence the process of seeking out the solutions which will resolve the obstacle.

Step 4: Subordinate Everything Else to the System Constraint

Using the tools of the TLS Continuum methodology it is time to turn to the DMAIC (Define-Measure-Analyze-Improve-Control) process and research our problem. Specifically, we take the goal from Step 1 and make that the problem. As in the scientific method, we then need to begin the process of measuring the problem. We want to identify whether what we think is going wrong is in fact the true cause of the problem. With the evidence-based metrics derived from the measurement stage we then analyze the metrics to see what the data is telling us.

Once the earlier stages are completed we then proceed to the last two stages. The purpose of this stage is to make the resolution of the problem the primary function of the organization.

Step 5: Elevate the Constraint

With the constraint (problem or obstacle) identified we then elevate the constraint so that we can cure the obstacle. At the same time, we want to create a standard of work and remove variations from the processes. Our intent is to ensure that we have remedied the obstacle and have the organization on the path to sustainable change management.

Step 6: Start the Process over Again by Identifying a New Constraint

The change management fact of life is that the above process does not rectify all the organizational obstacles. It is also true that once you resolve the one constraint another one will appear and then we will begin the process all over again. It is necessary that we take some time to discuss a dichotomy between two views of the change management arena.

The use of the Lean and Six Sigma methodology suggests that the new constraint will be apparent in approximately three to six months. This is instilled in every facilitator's presentations in this area. When we combine Lean and Six Sigma with the Theory of Constraints the new constraint should be visible immediately after we complete the process above.

The TLS Continuum can be better explained by stating its ultimate goal. We use TOC to identify the obstacles and then we use Lean to remove that obstacle and Six Sigma to create a standard of work and eliminate and control all variations from the organizational processes.

In my experience looking at organizational issues and my writings in my four previous titles it became apparent that there was something missing in the equation. Maybe not missing, but it was not clearly delineated. That missing element was the mechanism for empowering the organization to bring about the changes that are required to engage in continuous process improvement. The result was the development of the TLS Continuum Empowerment Model.

The TLS Continuum Empowerment Model

The TLS Continuum Empowerment Model looks at the organization and considers what determines the success of empowerment within that organization. The empowerment process is shown below in Figure 4.2.

The model consists of four levels, each being interdependent on the previous one for success. In Chapters 5–7 I will look at each level in more depth. Before we do that, I need to provide some context for the model structure going forward.

The initial level of the model is that of management empowerment. While it provides the basis for the model, it is not in my opinion the most important. It does however provide the organization with guides to the organizational mission, values, goals, culture and overall strategy. It basically sets the boundaries of the CPI throughout the organization. It should be noted here that in this VUCA age we are in, this does require a degree of flexibility in those boundaries. Management is the steering currents of the organization providing the organizational model for how things are supposed to operate.

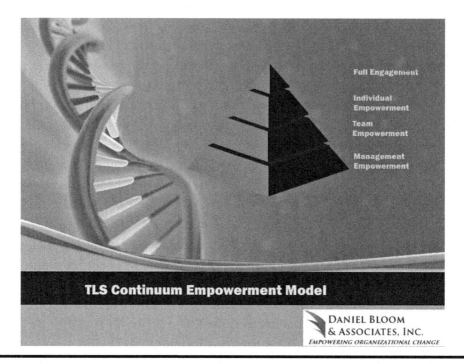

Figure 4.2 TLS Continuum Empowerment Model.

The management philosophy sends both visible and audible messages to the human capital assets on the direction that the organization is going.

The next level in the model is the role of cross-functional teams. They are the heart of the CPI efforts. In Chapter 6 we will look at some very specific requirements for the model to work in an organization. Suffice it to say at this juncture that there can be good teams and there can be bad teams. It all depends on how they are structured and run. The team must have clear guidance from management that their mission is not only wanted but accepted by the organization as a whole. They are the innovators who will guide the organization through the change process.

The third level is that of the individual human capital assets within the organization. It is my belief that this is the most important level in the model. This is where the human capital assets are instilled with the belief that their opinions matter. This is where the human capital assets understand that they are not just a number or a line in the organizational financial records. This is where they learn the power of one's ideas to enhance the organization going forward.

The fourth and final level of the model is total empowerment and engagement. It is where all the other three levels come together. It is where the combination changes the organization. It is where the stakeholders and the human capital assets and management come together in a new working relationship destined to carry the organization to new heights. I will explore that new work environment in Chapter 7.

In each of the following chapters I will explore these levels in more depth and discuss some benefits and drawbacks at each level where they exist. To better understand our journey going forward, place a paper clip on page 34 as we will build a Goal Tree map for the journey. Let's look at the beginning of that exercise.

TLS Continuum Empowerment Model Goal Tree

In order to have

> ### Total Empowerment and Engagement

I must have

> ### Empowered Management
> ### Empowered Cross-Functional Teams
> ### Empowered Human Capital Assets

Notes

1. Used with permission of Robert Sproull for his Focus and Leverage series of books.
2. Lawrence Miller is a college classmate. He originated the idea of the whole system architecture of an organization in his article "Whole System Architecture: A Model for Building the Lean Organization." www.lmmiller. com/wp-content/uploads/2011/06/Whole-System-Architecture-Article1.pdf
3. Dettmer, William. *The Logical Thinking Process*. Milwaukee, WI: ASQ Press, Pages 16–21.
4. Sproull, Robert. *Epiphanized 2nd Edition*. New York, NY: CRC Press, 2015. Pages 248–249.

Chapter 5

The Empowered Manager

In Figure 4.2, I presented the TLS Continuum Empowerment Model in the form of a pyramid. The base of the pyramid was empowered management. While in my mind it is not the most important segment of the pyramid, it does provide support and structure for the remaining segments. If you remember, both our formulas for empowerment and for continuous process improvement included a necessary ingredient—management style.

Neil Kokemuller suggests that,

> In an effective business, the role of management is clearly distinguished from that of front-line workers. Managers develop and communicate the overall purpose and structure of the company. Managers also build a collaborative company culture and team atmosphere that makes the line between management and employees closer.[1]

Dr. Rosabeth Kanter in her Theory on Structural Empowerment[2] suggests that management empowerment requires organizations to provide opportunities for advancement, access to information, access to support, access to resources, formal power and informal power. At no time does Dr. Kanter reference the role of the empowered human capital assets.

The classic organizational management or manager governs the organization from a top down model similar to the military. They decide the corporate policy and expect with the stroke of a pen or the utterance of some words that the organization will naturally fall in line with the transmission.

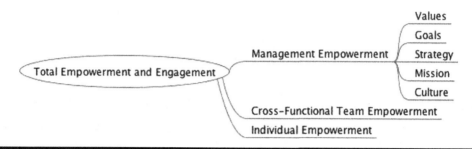

Figure 5.1 Management Empowerment.

From there the manager formulates the organizational mission, values, goals, strategy and the alignment of the organization.

The empowered manager provides the same set of ultimate policies but in cooperation with the other parts of the TLS Continuum Empowerment Model. From our perspective an empowered organizational management/ manager, as shown in Figure 5.1, provides the organization and its human capital assets with a standard set of values, defined corporate goals, defined strategy, a defined mission and an underlying corporate culture. It is critical to our discussion that you have a clear picture as to what each means in your organization.

Corporate Values

Corporate values—every organization has them. However, one set of values that is true for your organization may not be the same for the next organization that you are exposed to. The term corporate values mean many things to different people. The Business Dictionary defines corporate values as the operating philosophies or principles that guide an organization's internal conduct as well as its relationship with its customers, partners and shareholders.[3] These values are generally established by upper management. Your values may be routed in a religious belief such as Chick-Fil-A, which has made the business decision to close its stores on Sunday because of them. The values may be grounded in a philosophy of business as to how a company should be run. This wide divergence of value definitions can be found in HubSpot's list of top corporate values.[4] Consider some of these values from an empowerment focus:

Integrity – In order to empower the organization in the workplace, management needs to walk the walk and talk the talk in the integrity area. Consider this example where the organization did not follow the plan. At the suggestion of my college roommate I left teaching and became a contingency executive recruiter back in the early 1970s. Shortly thereafter the company opened a division in New York City. I was promoted to the position of vice president and was given the responsibility of discussing sourcing with members of the supply chain. If you know anything about the inner workings of the national CPA firms, you know there are always, on a yearly basis, the outsourcing of accountants who will not make partner. I met with the outsourcing director of one of these firms and we agreed that as long as the firm did not recruit the auditors away from the CPA clients, we would receive the names and backgrounds of those on the way out the door. I returned to the office and in a group meeting explained what was negotiated. Within half an hour one of the other recruiting banks did exactly what we said we would not do. When I brought it to the attention of my college roommate who was president of the new division, his response to the organization was that "if you had any business ethics, you did not belong at the firm." Obviously, to the supply chain in the marketplace, the company did not have any sense of integrity.

The empowered manager on the other hand will ensure that the integrity message is universal throughout the organization and to its stakeholders. They will not deliver one message to the organization and have a different message for the outside world, like my college roommate did.

Accountability – the empowered manager understands that there is a shared sense of accountability throughout the organization. The human capital assets are accountable to the organization for their work. The management is accountable to the human capital assets to deliver what they promise will be provided to them. Both parties in turn are accountable to the stakeholders to provide the services or products they have promised to them.

Commitment to Customers – The lifeblood of any organization is the customers they serve. The empowered manager understands this bedrock principle of business. The empowered manager as a result takes sincere steps to ensure that the organization delivers what they promise to those customers. The size of the customer makes no difference in the message. The empowered manager relays through their actions and words that they appreciate the value of the customers to the organization.

Constant Improvement – The empowered manager understands that there is no such thing as perfection. The only way for the organization to succeed is to constantly strive to make itself better. Better in the way it treats the stakeholders. Better in the way it delivers its services and products.

Better in the way it develops new products and services. As with integrity, the empowered manager must make the walk and the talk.

Leadership – There has been much written of late about the types of leadership required in our organizations. The empowered manager understands that in order for the organization to function at a certain level the leadership style must change. Whether you call this servant leadership or some other term of the day, the goal of the empowered manager is to guide the organization through a leadership model which supports everyone within the organization.

Teamwork – The empowered manager understands that the final performance results of the organization are a collective effort. As shown in the next chapter, there are certain criteria which enhance the power of the team. The important thing at this juncture is to understand that a true team is not a serfdom. The empowered manager understands that their purpose is to be the coach to the organization, not its dictator. While the management still has to lay out some guidelines, these guidelines cannot be the single factor in deciding whether the organization is successful.

Corporate Goals

Based on its corporate culture, mission statement and values, the organization establishes a strategy to ensure that it is on the right path to meet those statements of who the organization is. Every organization establishes a set of specific targets which determine whether the organization is on the right track. These targets are specific in time and place and they are quantifiable, meaning that we have verifiable data to support them. The empowered manager understands these targets and how to disseminate them to the organization. The empowered manager understands that these targets are not just some artificial thought or concept but a living embodiment of the organization. They are the lifeblood of the organization.

Corporate Strategy

The empowered manager, with the assistance of the entire organization, takes the goals and imports them into a statement of how you are going to achieve the goals. It sets out who is responsible for what part of the strategy and how you will prove that the goals have been achieved.

We can further demonstrate the path we are on by using a goals tree as discussed earlier in this work. The empowered manager understands that in order to have an empowered organization, the management must also be empowered. Their sense of empowerment comes from the total system in which they are embedded. This total system is described as a whole system architecture as defined in an article by Dr. Lawrence Miller on the topic.[5] Their empowerment comes from the human capital assets, the stakeholders, the customers and the supply chain that feeds the organization. The empowered manager understands that the world has changed, and that top down oversight is no longer effective in this multi-generational world we are in. The empowered manager understands that while they have the responsibility to guide the discussion regarding corporate values, goals, mission and culture they are not the primary force behind them. As we will see in Chapter 6, the net level of the pyramid, the empowered cross-functional team, will be the driver behind much of this effort.

Corporate Mission

Based on the corporate culture definition, the organization through its mission statement goes on to identify who the organization is and who their basic clients are. The empowered manager assists the organization in not only delineating the mission statement but the implementation of it in real time.

Corporate Culture

According to the website Investopedia, the term corporate culture refers to the beliefs and behaviors that determine how a company's employees and management interact and handle outside business transactions.[6] As indicated by Investopedia, the corporate culture is the foundation of the organization and everything else feeds off this cultural statement.[7]

TLS Continuum Empowerment Model Goal Tree

In order to have

Total Empowerment and Engagement

I must have

Empowered Management

In order to have

Empowered Management

I must have

A Set of Corporate Values
Established Corporate Goals
Established Corporate Strategies
Established Corporate Mission
Established Corporate Culture

Notes

1. Kokemuller, Neil. "Brief Description of the Role of Management in an Organization." AZCentral.com https://yourbusiness.azcentral.com/brief-description-role-management-organization-22173.html
2. Kanter, Rosabeth. "Overview of Kanter's Theory on Structural Empowerment." https://structuralempowerment.weebly.com/kaneters-theory.htm
3. https://blog.hubspot.com/marketing/company-values
4. Miller, Lawrence. "Whole-System Architecture: A Model for Building a Lean Organization." www.lmmiller.com/wp-content/uploads/2011/06/Whole-System-Architecture-Article1.pdf
5. Miller, Lawrence. "Whole-System Architecture: A Model for Building a Lean Organization." www.lmmiller.com/wp-content/uploads/2011/06/Whole-System-Architecture-Article1.pdf
6. Business Dictionary. Definition of Corporate Values. www.businessdictionary.com/definition/corporate-values.html
7. www.investopedia.com/terms/c/corporate-culture.asp

Chapter 6

Empowerment through Cross-Functional Teams

The next level in the TLS Continuum Empowerment Model pyramid is that of the role of cross-functional teams. If you look at the business world the subject of business teams is a major area of concern. How do we construct them? Who should be part of them? What do we do with the result of the work of the team? Google the term "business teams," and it results in 1,210,000,000 items. If we change the search criteria to ask for "business team books," the result is 223,000,000 titles. If we turn to the websites of Amazon and Barnes & Noble and ask them to search for business teams, we get 30,000 and 360 titles, respectively.

Obviously, the concept of workplace teams is a point of critical discussion. The real question becomes how they operate within our workplaces. In this chapter I will look at the creation of teams historically and then compare the classic concept of teams and empowered teams.

One of the meeting programs that I present is titled "Who Am I? The Role of Human Capital Assets in the Global Workplace" in which we present the fact that teams, either formally or informally, have been around since the 1700s, the first teams being the family farm and the way in which the family worked as a team to complete necessary tasks.

In 1909, with the publication of his *Principles of Scientific Management,* Frederick Winslow Taylor first introduced the idea that workers and managers need to cooperate with each other. From this idea Taylor began a series of Time and Motion studies to discover how to more effectively run the workplace.

These studies resulted in Taylor's Four Principles of Scientific Management.[1] In his first principle Taylor advocated that organizations should replace working by "rule of thumb," and instead use the scientific method to study work and determine how most efficiently to perform specific tasks. In other words, Taylor suggested that we actually have a process to complete a task. The second principle suggested a different way of assigning tasks. Rather than simply assigning workers to any job, we should assign workers based on capability and motivation. One of the tenets of my "The Road to HR Excellence through Six Sigma" course is that team members should be selected based on their skills and attitudes. From this point Taylor, in his third principle, suggested that the performance of workers should be monitored and that they should be provided with instructions and supervision to ensure that they are using the most efficient ways of working. This principle reinforces the Toyota premise of the manager as a coach. The final principle advocated that the work between managers and workers be allocated so that the workers were allowed to perform their tasks efficiently. I will discuss this last principle more in depth in the next chapter. The drawback to these principles is that are based on the idea that there is only one way to do something and that does not allow for innovation or expanded views of the problem.

Hawthorne Studies

Sixty-one years later, with the Principles of Scientific Management embedded into the global business workplace, a team of Harvard business professors (Elton May, F.J. Roethlisberger and William J. Dickinson) were contracted by Western Electric to conduct a series of studies at their Hawthorne plant in Cicero, Illinois. The initial scope of the studies was concentrated on the physical and environmental issues surrounding the plant and its effect on the human capital assets.

Shortly after beginning the Hawthorne studies, the Harvard business professors discovered that in addition to the physical and environmental issues, there was a social issue to the workings of the Cicero plant.

Mayo et al. looked at the social dynamics of the groups within the plant. Like Frederick Taylor they discovered that the relationships between supervisors and workers govern the success of the team. They further expressed the view that the workplace is a social system made up of many parts. These social dynamics have a direct correlation to the total productivity of the organization.

However, we had heard this concept before from Abraham Maslow who, in his Hierarchy of Needs, suggested that the third level of the pyramid was the need for belongingness and love. To carry this forward, it is that need for belongingness which empowers organizational teams.

Our organizations are confronted with a choice. They can continue in their time-tested mode or create a new paradigm for team construction. The rest of this chapter will show the difference between the two types of teams. It is worth mentioning at this juncture that Robert Mathis in his seminal work *Human Resource Management* suggests that in every organization there exists three types of teams—special purpose teams, self-directed teams and virtual teams.[2] Our concentration in this book is primarily centered on the self-directed teams, although the same principles can be applied to all of them.

Classical Workplace Teams

I would expect that everyone reading this book has at one time or another served on a team within their workplace. I would also expect that many of these teams fit the model of the classical team.

Classical workplace teams, no matter what type they are, are constructed identically. Management asks certain members of the organization to be part of a team designed to solve a particular problem that confronts the organization. The typical team is comprised of a member of management and possibly 5–8 individuals from the rest of the organization. They come together periodically to discuss the nature of the problem and possible solutions.

From the teams that I have been part of during my half century business career, they almost always work the same way. We gather around a table and the management representative asks for our suggestions and then management decides the solution. Or after the end of the discussions the team decides to experience "groupthink," and everyone condescends round a single solution whether it is the best solution or not.

Groupthink presents the classical team and your organization with a double-edged sword. From one side Groupthink provides a relatively swift way to resolve process problems. The team tends to use lateral thinking to look at the problem in the light of previous problems and tries to apply the same logic as the previous problem to the new situation. It is valid to point out that there is a form of synergy among team members involved and that sense of synergy comes from the preliminary sharing of information among team members. The presence of group-think can also contribute to the presence of management control of the process. As I will show below, the over-managing of a team is not the way you empower cross-functional teams. Safi Bahcall, in his book *Loonshots*, describes these actions and falling in to two traps:[3] The Moses Trap, in which the manager listens to the possible solutions and decides which solution will be implemented; and the PARC trap in which the solutions are totally disregarded, the very situation I discussed in *Reality, Perception and Your Company's Workplace Culture* when I talked about the difference between recognizing a problem and determining that there is nothing there.

One of these developments was created by Karoru Ishikawa. This current development we are referring to is the concept of "Quality Circles." The first organization to utilize Quality Circles was Nippon Wireless and Telegraph starting about a decade after the introduction of Deming's work in Japan. Quality Circles functioned, essentially, the same regardless of the company's organizational structure.

The concept behind the operation of Quality Circles was that it was comprised of small groups of managers and employees who voluntarily got together to solve intercompany problems. The members were trained in the tenets of statistical process control, giving them the basis for identifying and analyzing processes within the organization. The meetings were held around the normal work schedule, occurring either during lunch breaks or before or after work. It should be noted that the solutions were designed to handle issues ranging from safety and health to product design and manufacturing process improvements, so we are not talking about large scale problems. Further, despite the principles set forth by Deming, the Circles were more than likely within the same department or silo. Once a solution is developed it is presented to management for permission to implement the steps to change the process. After gaining management approval the solution is implemented. In some cases the members of the Quality Circle are awarded bonuses based on the amount of savings generated by their solutions.

The box below provides you the reader with a simple overview of their operations.

HUMAN RESOURCE EXCELLENCE 101: QUALITY CIRCLES

Mary Johnson has been a member of the human resource function at Excellence Manufacturing for nearly 15 years. One day she is reviewing an e-mail from a department manager, in which they are lamenting the length of time it takes to obtain approval for a new hire to take place. Mary talks with both the manager and some of her fellow department members to determine where the process is breaking down.

Based on the conversations, the people directly involved decide they will try and improve the process. The team consists of Mary, two of her fellow HR team members and the department manager. They begin to meet once a week after hours to look at the current process. From their review they identify what the problems are, select the final issue that needs to be resolved and analyze the impact of the problem on overall operations.

Following the completion of their studies they compile a report on the problem that was identified and the recommended solution and present their report to the organizational management team. Management, after the review of the completed project, gives the team the go ahead to implement the solution.

Their solution decreased the new hire process, saving the organization approximately $100,000 in costs. In turn the Quality Circle members received a 2 percent bonus in their pay due to their efforts.

In 1972, based on the success of Quality Circles in Japan, the improvement staff at Lockheed Space Missile Factory in California brought them to the United States. Japanese organizations demonstrated that the Circles brought about major changes in their organizations. The interest came about after aerospace representatives visited an assortment of Japanese manufacturing facilities and saw the Quality Circles in operation.

As can be seen from the description above, the quality circles were the perfect example of the classical team format. While the other members of the team arrived at solutions, it was left up to management to decide whether the solutions were implemented or discarded. General Electric under Jack Welsh saw the folly in this method, and they implemented the GE Workout and the Change Acceleration Process (CAP) to counter the classical team outcomes.

Do not construe from the discussion that I am totally against classical teams. They have their place and purpose. If you are trying to decide whether to purchase a supply of copy paper or whether to purchase office services, the need might not be there for the scope of problem solutions I am discussing in the empowered team section below. And that is fine.

The other side of the double-edged sword is the negatives of the classical cross-functional team. The classical cross-functional team is characterized by a command and control process. The downside is represented by several outcomes. First, when you sidetrack team members' views it can ruin relationships that have been developed within your organization. In her writings, Adrienne Rich said,

> when those who have the power to name, and to socially construct reality choose not to see you or hear you, ... when someone with the authority of a teacher say, describes the world and you are not in it, there is a moment of psychic disequilibrium, as if you looked into a mirror and saw nothing.[4]

The classical team runs the risk of having team members who feel like the person in Adrienne Rich's poem. The argument is that your views are not valid because the management-controlled view is considered the majority opinion of the group.

The second downside is that because ideas are discarded the ability to potentially find a breakthrough solution is sometimes overlooked. The tendency is that if the problem resembles a previous problem, why not use that solution in the current situation? The result is that not all the available solutions are considered.

The third downside is that false decisions have a tendency to lower the quality of the process and the organization. The classical cross-functional teams tend to try and assume what the voice of the customer is saying even if the true nature of the problem is misunderstood by the team. Remember that in the Six Sigma end of the spectrum we don't know what we don't know. The result is that the team takes on a false sense of security by believing that the right choice has been made when in fact we have left out some part of the equation in arriving at the conclusion.

One of the biggest downsides, not only with classical cross-functional teams but further with the HR function as a whole, is that many of today's professionals either were never taught or have forgotten what it means to critically think through daily challenges. If they were never taught, it is the fault of the educational system; if they forgot how to use those skills it is because they have never been asked to do so in their organization. As we will see below the empowered cross-functional team demands that we critically think through the problems that confront us.

Another downside is that due to the way classical cross-functional teams operate, there is an inherent lack of engagement. The teams believe that they are invulnerable and can do no wrong. They are the masters of knowledge of the organizational processes. This leads, as we suggested above, to the idea that they are always right, that their beliefs should not be questioned. The beliefs are required to be inside a mindset designed to ensure that the corporate culture is not challenged even if that means that you are making a decision that may harm the organization or the client.

Empowered Workplace Teams

Unlike the classical team, the empowered team is a whole new look for the organization. It looks to take advantage of the best resources to resolve organizational issues based on the voice of the customer. It expands the focus of the organization into new areas. It adds new resources that are often overlooked by the classical teams. In the pages that follow I will look at each of these added views in more detail.

As can be seen in Figure 6.1, the empowered team must view its purpose from the view of diversity of ideas, full spectrum thinking, new decision tools and the method by which we construct teams.

Diversity

Is your organization one of those involved in a diversity campaign? Does your management team include a Chief Diversity and Inclusion Officer? If so, you are among the numerous organizations that have picked up on this

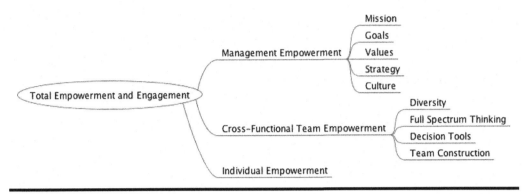

Figure 6.1 Team Empowerment.

trend. The goal behind these efforts is to move towards the inclusion of multiple backgrounds within the organization, both educationally and ethically. I agree with the assessment that it is a critical issue, but we are looking at a different type of diversity. I am looking at the idea of diversity in a different light.

Diversity in the empowered team arena looks at who is included in the deliberations. In any organization, there exists a spectrum of thought, if you will. To completely resolve the issues confronting the organization, it is necessary that you include everyone who touches the problem in any way or manner. So, who I am talking about? Consider as you construct your teams the entire supply chain from start to finish. Consider the problem I discussed in *Reality, Perception and Your Company's Workplace Culture.* Your major customer says that the product or service you are delivering to them fails to meet their needs and they are threatening to take their business elsewhere. The question is: Who do you call first? You want to reach out to everyone involved in the production of that product or service at both ends of the spectrum.

Take for example the car you drive. Who touches that automobile even remotely in getting the car to you? You have all the parts in the car, each made by a separate supplier. You have all the suppliers that service the part supplier, and you have all their suppliers. Once the car is assembled at the plant, you then have the supplier who delivers the car to your dealership. After delivery, you have whoever services the vehicle when it needs maintenance. This is the concept behind the consideration of stakeholders versus shareholders.

Let's review for a moment the difference between the two. Many corporations contend that their purpose is to meet the needs of their shareholders.

First let me make it abundantly clear that all shareholders are in themselves stakeholders. The difference is that their involvement in the organization is purely financial in nature.

R. Edward Freeman suggests that there exists an interconnected relationship between a business and its customers, suppliers, employees, investors, communities and others who have a stake in the organization. The theory argues that a firm should create value for all stakeholders, not just shareholders.[5] Accepting the narrow view of meeting the needs of the shareholders versus the stakeholders provides you with a narrow field of thinking about the problem. It tends to leave out the possibility of breakthrough solutions. The stakeholder theory talks about the community. I would suggest that community should also include openness to outside solutions, as we discuss in the next section. In their book *New Power*, Jeremy Heimans and Henry Timms suggest one characteristic of the new business world is the need for collaboration. Millennials have no hesitation in jumping on their computer and asking for assistance from whoever in order to resolve a problem. NASA used the power of a site called InnoCentive[6] to resolve problems that the in-house experts could not.

The empowered team will ensure that the solution that is arrived at includes the widest spectrum of thought regarding the issue at hand. It needs to identify and include the openness to diverse thoughts on the solution. Not the confined view of most organizations.

So how do you identify these stakeholders? One of the easiest methods is to use a SIPOC form,[7] which I discussed in our *Achieving HR Excellence through Six Sigma* course. The tool shown on the next page consists of five columns and is completed by initially defining the process involved. From there we work left to right and complete each column. The easiest method to do this is look at the process and ask yourself who are your suppliers and what do they contribute (inputs) to the process. Most process improvement professionals will tell you that you want to limit the number of sources to the top five. For this exercise I would counter that you want to identify as many sources as possible. With the first three columns completed you then want to identify the outputs for each source. When they make the contribution to the process, what does the process generate for the end user? The final column is who the product or service is delivered to.

I know if you completed one of these you would have put a fair amount of time into the task. But for our purposes in this book, you need to concentrate your time on the first and last columns.

SIPOC Diagram

Template Provided by Bright Hub Project Management

Suppliers	Input	Process	Output	Customers

The two columns define who your stakeholders are. Sadi Bahcall, in his book *Loonshots*, suggests that the magical number for team size is 150 members.[8] I totally understand that having 150 individuals in one room at the same time and expecting to get anything done is a bit unreal. What I am suggesting is that, as needed, the stakeholders can be rotated in and out of the problem-solving process as they are needed.

The takeaway from this idea is that the solutions to today's problems are centered in the VUCA age we are in. The work environment is subject to volatility because circumstances can change on the flip of a coin. This volatility brings a wide degree of uncertainty into the way our processes behave. The combination of volatility and uncertainty means that the work-place is in constant chaos. Further, the sense of ambiguity means that what we think is the answer may not be the answer. Stakeholders bring into the picture the potential for innovative and strong answers to problems. Marshall Goldsmith's seminal book *What Got You Here Won't Get You There* provides the answer for your empowered teams. The stakeholders provide the guidance to get us there. However, not if we do things in the same way we always have. The next section is a look at the first way we get there.

Full Spectrum Thinking

In part, this VUCA age is based in what Michael Hayden in his book *The Assault on Intelligence* refers to as an era of post-truth.[9] It is an era where we base our decisions on personal beliefs and appeals to emotions. In my nearly 50 years in the business world, I have seen this play out on numerous occasions. If something goes wrong in the office, it is always the employee's fault. A customer complains something is wrong with an order; it is the employee's fault, so you fire them. It is an age where we make decisions at the expense of facts and data. There is a solution to this dilemma, and it is called full spectrum thinking.

What is full spectrum thinking you may ask? Throughout my writings I have talked about seeing a problem, feeling a problem and changing the corporate culture. One aspect of that concept is that we have to exercise our power of judgment in order to think. Daniel Kahneman, a Professor of Psychology and Public Affairs Emeritus at the Woodrow Wilson School, the Eugene Higgins Professor of Psychology Emeritus at Princeton University and a fellow of the Center for Rationality at the Hebrew University in Jerusalem, in 2011 presented his views on business decision making in his book *Thinking Fast and Slow*[10] in which he suggested that we need to make our decisions based on two levels.

Kahneman refers to the first level as System 1 Thinking. I use this form of thinking every day, both personally and professionally. You use this form of thinking every day personally and professionally. It inspires quick response decisions.

The base of the system is emotional. When was the last time you got near a hot stove and jerked your hand back? When was the last time that you needed to order a resupply of, say, copy paper and you just went online and ordered it? These are examples of System 1 thinking. We find System 1 very prevalent in the groupthink workplaces where the power of the organization rests in the hands of the management. The decisions are made based on past experiences and memories. As we stated earlier when you have a process problem you determine the solution based on similar events from the past. You almost automatically determine that because something worked in a similar situation in the past, the same solution should work in this situation. It seemingly works because it takes no effort to make the decision.

System 2 thinking is slower, more methodical in nature. System 2 thinking requires us to critically think about a solution. It asks us to take into consideration that just because the solution in front of us sounds right, it may not be the best solution to fit the problem. Think about the last time you had a problem to resolve. Was it easy to resolve the issues? My guess is probably not.

The further we get away from picking up the telephone or from hitting a key on the keyboard, the more the solution requires multiple aspects to resolve the problem. The more complex the solution, the more the demand for further investigation. Astrid Groenewegen and Tom de Bruyne, founders of SUE Behavioural Design, created a quick study guide to the differences between System 1 and System 2 thinking.[11] While my intent is not to redo their quick study guide, I do want to take place some added emphasis from several aspects of the System 2 thinking as it applies to the question of empowered teams.

One of the basic principles of the TLS Continuum is that our solutions are based on credible and verifiable data. The System 2 side of the spectrum is based on evidence not on thoughts. Consider this scenario. On one hand you determine a solution to a problem by saying, well when we have had similar issues in the past this is the way we resolved them; or we have a problem how can we determine what the causes are? The latter scenario used to resolve the issue is influenced by facts, logic and evidence. It is ingrained in intentional thinking rather than intuition. The empowered team performs its "experiments" to arrive at the correct solutions. The reasons behind the selection of a particular solution are based on the conscious reasoning abilities of the team. System 2 thinking comes into play whenever you do not have the conditions present to make a quick decision. I would suggest that other than ordering new supplies or some minor issue with a product or service, the TLS Continuum Empowerment Model would expect that System 2 thinking would be the standard problem-solving method. Full spectrum thinking requires the empowered cross-functional team to weigh up all the available options. The empowered team understands that to find the right solution there must be a change in the way we approach organizational problems. Part of that is the introduction of new decision tools.

New Decision Tools

The Theory of Constraints, Lean and Six Sigma; each in its own right offers your organization a set of tools. This Six Sigma Toolbox is as shown below. Note that the toolbox covers both the Lean tools and the Six Sigma tools. The Lean toolbox should be your first call in solving the problem. They are usually the low hanging fruit solutions (Figure 6.2).

In the book *Achieving HR Excellence through Six Sigma*, I discussed many of these tools in more detail. However, the Theory of Constraints

DMAIC Step	SIX SIGMA Tools	LEAN Tools
DEFINE	Voice of Customer Project Charter Project Critical to Quality Definition High Level Process Map	Value Definition
MEASURE	Quality Function Deployment Measurement System Analysis	Value Stream Mapping
ANALYZE	Process Capability Analysis FMEA Benchmarking Hypothesis Testing Graphical Tools	Line Balance Takt Time Calculation
IMPROVE	Regression Analysis Design Of Experiments Risk Assessment	5 S Establish Flow / Pull System SCORE Events
CONTROL	Determine New Process Capability Statistical Process Control Control Plans	Poke Yoke Visual Management

Figure 6.2   Lean Six Sigma Toolbox.

brings its own critical thinking tools to the table. An in-depth discussion of these tools can be found in H. William Dettmer's *The Logical Thinking Process.*

While there are a number of tools in the TOC critical thinking process as Dettmer describes, for our purposes I want to concentrate on two of the tools at this juncture. The Goal Tree and the Conflict Resolution Tree.

The Goal Tree

The Goal Tree is a clear method to demonstrate the empowerment of the team. The team is constructed and then they begin to deliberate over the questions that we get from the design thinking field. The beginning is asking the question "what is?" which represents the problem or goal. As can be seen in Figure 6.3, once the goal or problem is in place the next question is: In order to reach the goal what are the critical factors that must be in place? With the critical success factors in place, your next task is to determine what the necessary conditions are that must be in place for the critical factors to be created. You would do this for each of the critical factors in your journey to the goal.

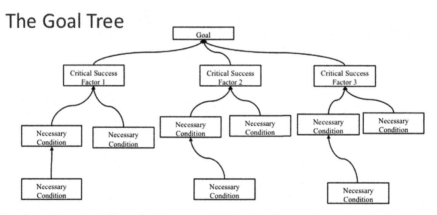

- The Goal sits at the top with the Critical Success Factors (CSFs) lying immediately below the Goal and the relevant Necessary Conditions (NCs) immediately beneath the CSF's.

- The CSFs are limited to no more than 3-5 in number and the layers of NCs are typically no more than three.

- The real value of the Goal Tree is to keep the analysis focused on what's really important to system success.

Figure 6.3   The Goal Tree.

The purpose of this book is not to discuss the tool in great detail, as Dettmer's *The Logical Thinking Process* goes into full chapters just on this tool. In addition, I would refer you to Bob Sproull's *The Focus and Leverage Improvement Book.* On pages 68–90 Bob lays out a simulation of a team creating The Goal Tree.

Another powerful aspect of The Goal Tree is the ability go back to your completed goal tree and develop the performance metrics for the process by asking yourself what does the successful achievement of each level mean to the organization. The procedure is you reverse the arrows on the diagram to run from the bottom up to the goal. At each level you ask yourself what would tell you that you have the right conditions in place. For example, you need to fill your hiring needs and one of the necessary conditions is that you have qualified individuals in the pipeline. What would tell you that they are qualified individuals? What would they look like?

The Evaporating Cloud or Conflict Resolution

The second tool from the Theory of Constraints toolbox of interest here is the Evaporating Cloud or the Conflict Resolution Tree. The Evaporating Cloud is designed to uncover the conflict within your processes. Consider for a moment the example in Figure 6.4. It states that one of HR's

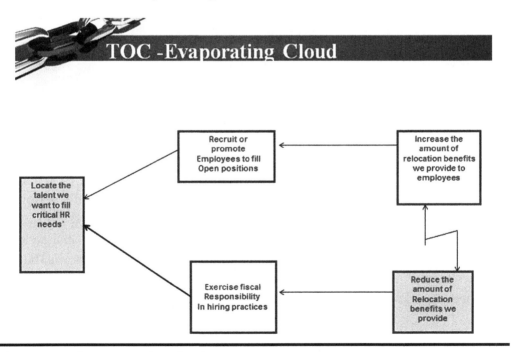

Figure 6.4   The Evaporating Cloud.

responsibilities is to locate the talent the organization needs to fill critical human capital needs of the organization. The question posed by the Evaporating Cloud is: How do we achieve that goal? The cloud offers two different alternatives. One says the goal is fiscal responsibility, which requires the organization to stay within budgetary guidelines. The other option states that the goal is to recruit or promote employees to fill these critical openings.

The weakest link appears after this segment of the discussion because it directly compares the two approaches. On the fiscal side, the resulting action is to reduce the amount of relocation benefits provided to the human capital assets, while filling the positions is the paramount issue you need to increase the level of benefits. The conflict arises because you may not be able to reduce benefits and still get the level of talent that the organization is seeking. The Evaporating Cloud contains three parts. The first is the objective or the problem/goal. This is supported by both a requirement (Critical Success Factor) and a Prerequisite (Necessary Condition). Much like the Goal Tree the CRT is read for each branch that in order to have your goal we must have requirement 1 in place. In order to have requirement 1 in place we must have prerequisite 1 in place. The conflict is created when prerequisites 1 and 2 are in conflict.

Steven Johnson in his book *Farsighted* suggests some additional tools that the empowered team can utilize to enhance your organization.

Mapping

I am sure that most of you have had experience with process maps or value stream maps, but this tool goes beyond those mapping exercises. Here I am referring to the use of mind mapping efforts. My two favorites are Free Mind and Draw, IO. You saw examples of mind maps in Figure 6.1.

The process is that the team begins with a parent node which represents your problem. From the parent node you brainstorm the potential solutions to the problem. Each "what if?" solution is represented by a sibling node. You can continue to add to the chart as you come up with additional factors that contribute to the issue resolution. The benefit of the mind map is that it allows for the introduction of alternative solutions that otherwise might have been overlooked. There is no such thing as a dumb solution suggestion here, your goal is to arrive at the broadest array of possible solutions that may or may not have a bearing on the problem. You want to make sure that the mind maps are shared with all the stakeholders. This sharing effort must allow for the stakeholders' input as to problems with the proposed solutions and any additional solutions they see that you forgot.

Premortem

The second tool is the use of premortem, if you will. The third question of the design thinking methodology is the answer to the question of "What Works?" Do not be afraid of the risk of failure. The idea is to take the more promising solutions and try them out with a narrow set of stakeholders to see if the proposed solutions accurately work in real time. This does not mean that you turn to stakeholders and ask them if they think the solution will work; you actually set up a demo model of your solution and let them take it for a test run. Let them help you find the flaws in the solution. Let them provide you with a good and bad analysis of the solution.

Solutions

The final tool is the determination of the solution menu to resolve the issue at hand. All too often we rush to a judgment as to a solution. It comes from the use of the first idea that comes to mind. It comes from a view that this is what we should do. Francesca Gino, in her article for the Harvard Business Press, suggests that the right question to ask is not what we should do but rather what could we do.[12] Changing the focus from "should" to "could do" opens the discussion to more creative suggestions for applicable solutions, especially in light of what we discussed above, that part of the success of the empowered team is collaboration. So if you go out to the wide range of ideas, the "could do" mode allows for more inclusion of the diversity of ideas on the market.

Team Construction

The last subject that I need to discuss in summarizing the empowered team level of the TLS Continuum Empowerment Model is to discuss the construction of the teams themselves. As referred to earlier, Sadi Bahcall in his book *Loonshots* suggested that the magic number for a team is 150 members. Before you start shouting that is absurd, I agree with you, but there is a better method that can be implemented here.

The team should start out with a core constituency. This is not necessarily exact persons but rather the functions they play. I would suggest that every team should contain representatives from management, HR, finance, sales, customer service, logistics and the floor manager. It is important to stress here that no member of this core is empowered to revert to command and control environments. The chosen solutions are the compilation of the ideas of the whole team not a team of one. Notice I am referring to a team of seven in the core. So where are the other 143 members?

John Ricketts in his book *Reaching the Goal*[13] suggests the creation of a talent bench. The rest of the 143 team members are rotated in and out of the team as their particular skills are needed. Once they have made their contribution they are rotated back to their normal duties. The process enhances the outcomes by utilizing the strongest human assets in the development of the solutions.

To summarize where we are at this point before moving on to what I believe is the most important part of the TLS Continuum Empowerment Model, we have looked at the role of both management and the cross-functional teams in the model. The management level, while representing the largest level, serves as the basis for the model, but their contribution is to establish the whys for the organization to exist through the implementation of goals, missions and values aligned with the organization strategies. The "how to" for the alignment strategies comes from the power of the empowered cross-functional teams as we have discussed in this chapter. But the key to all of this is in the next level of the pyramid—the role of the empowered individual.

TLS Continuum Empowerment Model Goal Tree

In order to have

Total Empowerment and Engagement

I must have

Empowered Management

In order to have

Empowered Management

I must have

Set of Corporate Values
Established Corporate Goals
Established Corporate Strategies
Established Corporate Mission
Established Corporate Culture

In order to have

Empowered Teams

I must have

Diversity
Full Spectrum Thinking
Decision Tools
Established Cross-Functional Teams

Notes

1. Mindtools. Frederick Taylor and Scientific Management. https://mindtool.com/pages/article/new/TMM_Taylor.htm
2. Mathis, Robert et al. *Human Resource Management*, Twelfth Edition. Mason, OH: Thomson South-West: 2008. Pages 168–169.
3. Bahcall, Sadi. *Loonshots*. New York, NY: St Martin's Press, 2019. Page 148.
4. Rich, Adrienne. *Blood, Bread, and Poetry: Selected Prose*, 1979–1985.
5. Freeman, R. Edward. *The Stakeholder Theory*. http://stakeholdertheory.org/about/
6. Epstein, David. *Range: Why Generalists Triumph in a Specialized World*. New York, NY: Riverhead Books, 2019. Pages 177–178.
7. https://www.brighthubpm.com/templates-forms/6179-ten-free-six-sigma-templates-you-can-download/
8. Bahcall, Sadi. *Loonshots*. New York, NY: St Martin's Press, 2019. Pages 199–202.
9. Hayden, Michael. *The Assault on Intelligence*. New York, New York: Penguin Press, 2018. Page 3.
10. Daniel Kahneman. *Thinking Fast and Slow*. Farrar, Straus and Giroux, 2011.
11. Groenewegen, Astrid, and de Bruyne, Tom. System Thinking Quick Study Guide. https://SUEbehaviouraldesign.com/sytem-1-2-quickguide/
12. Gino, Francesca. "When Solving Problems, Think about What You Could Do, Not What You Should Do." *Harvard Business Review*. https://hbr.org/2018/04/when-solving-problems-think-about-what-you-could-do-not-what-you-should-do
13. Ricketts, John. *Reaching the Goal: How Managers Improve a Services Business Using Goldratt's Theory of Constraints*. New York, NY: IBM Press, 2008.

Chapter 7

Empowerment of Human Capital

The third level of the TLS Continuum Empowerment Model is represented by the smallest of the three levels in the pyramid but is critically the most important. It is shown as the last level of the Empowerment mind map and represents the contributions of the individual human capital assets to the organization.

It is critical that we recognize that the human capital assets within our organization represent the organizational lifeblood and therefore represent the core of the organizational DNA—Empowerment. There is no organization in the global marketplace that can survive without the presence of human capital assets. They are the ones who implement the organization's values. They are the ones who interact with the organizational customers. They are the ones who present the image of the organization in the marketplace. They are the ones who fulfill the customer orders. They are the ones who disseminate the expanse of the corporate knowledge database to the newly acquired talent.

The third level of the TLS Continuum Empowerment Model pyramid, as shown in Figure 4.2, is that of the empowered individual. This does not represent the largest level in size, but from our perspective it represents the most important one. It represents the lifeblood of the organization. Take a moment and look at your organization, with an open mind, and respond to this question: How does your organization categorize your human capital assets? Do not jump to conclusions as to what the right answer is, as you might very well be wrong in your response. Your direct responses to the question determine whether you have empowered human capital assets or not within your organization.

Classic Human Capital Asset

As we approached the end of the 1700s our human capital assets began to feel the impact of the volatile, uncertain and chaotic world. The crop yields from year to year were shifting, making it hard to maintain a stable standard of living. The price that could be obtained for their crops depended on the market requests for what they were producing. Environmental conditions also affected their crops, whether these be weather related, or pest related. The solution that many families chose was to move to a big city where the opportunity for more stable employment and more stable lives was inherent.

As we reached the 1800s the human capital assets began an exodus to the large cities, such as New York, in search of more opportunities for a better life for their families. This exodus created the beginning of the industrial age in our history. The industrial age came about because our human capital assets wanted more from life than hours working off the land. They were looking to provide for their families. But in doing so the nature of work changed. Instead of being their own boss and controlling their work hours, they now reported to managers who oversaw the work. Management was more concerned with the bottom line in the form of profits, so wages were kept low. While the agricultural age human capital assets were used to long hours, in the new industrial age the human capital assets were asked to work 14 to 16-hour shifts, in working environments with poor lighting and ventilation. In the course of their shift there was little concern for worker safety, and they got a break for lunch and dinner. Above I asked you to take a moment and look at your organization, with an open mind, and respond to this question: How does your organization categorize your human capital assets? The answer to the question is that the individual employee became relegated to an object. They became classified as an expense item, exempt versus non-exempt (i.e. worker versus management). With the exception of the Cadbury Chocolate Company, who invented the Quaker Business Model[1], our human capital assets got rendered to just a number. Cadbury believed in helping out its human capital assets by offering programs that helped ensure the best in the individual was cultivated. But for the most part as stated, and to a great degree the same is true today, our human capital assets are identified by this magical number. The human capital assets became Adrienne Rich's person who looked in the mirror and saw nothing. The human capital assets were viewed as occupying a time and place assigned the task to build the organization's products.

As an expense item, the notion on the part of management was that if there were cost cutting needed, just lay off a few human capital assets. If the organization found it had extra staff based on customer demand, cut staffing levels. The notion that the individual human capital assets could make a significant contribution to the organization was a foreign language to many management members. The only part of the organization that knew and understood the organization was management and therefore the modus operandi for the organization was control and command. Management told the human capital assets that this was what was needed to be done, how it was to be done and when it was to be done by. It was not the role of human capital assets to offer alternative views of the processes. Their role was to do what was demanded by management. Management structured compensation packages based on the number of pieces each human capital asset produced during their shift.

Empowered Human Capital Asset

In 1969 on a global basis this new tool came into existence called the Internet. The direct result of this new tool was a dramatic evolution of the workplace. The workplace shifted from the conditions of the industrial age to what now was referred to as the information age. This essential understanding is the crux of the creation of the empowered human capital asset. Figure 7.1 displays those areas that will be discussed in this chapter.

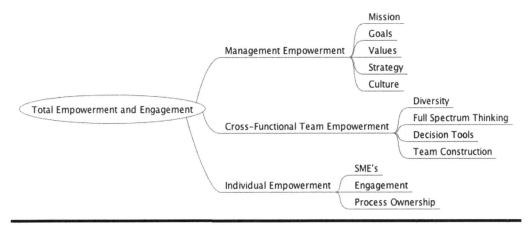

Figure 7.1   Human Capital Empowerment.

Russ Moen, Vice President, Human Resources at Express Services, Inc., explains the response to my question as to how you categorize your human capital assets in a slide from one of his programs as shown in Figure 7.2. As we moved from the farm to the factory floor it became the norm for our human capital assets to be identified by a number. Look at your company identification badge—you are probably still provided a unique number to locate you in corporate records. This worked for a while. As long as our human capital assets were paid based on the hours worked and the number of pieces made, the number system worked fine. But times would change and so would the nature of the role of the individual within the workplace, globally and internally.

Russ Moen makes the argument that, as an organization, we now compensate our human capital assets based not on what they make, but on what they dream. We do not employ the human capital assets to fill time and space. We hire them to derive new ideas, concepts and processes designed to meet the needs of the customer. The knowledge of what the organization does now resides in their heads. Example in point: Not too long ago a company wanted to reduce its overheads, so it offered every employee with 20 or more years of service an early buyout. Every one of them took the offer.

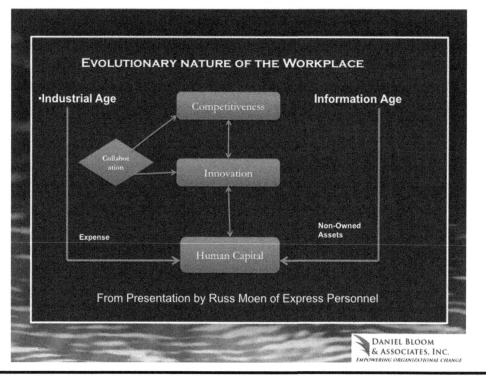

Figure 7.2   Evolutionary Nature of the Workplace[2].

The company was out of business in six months mostly due to the loss of knowledge within the company. Moen goes on to suggest that in the knowledge age, today's human capital assets are non-owned, corporate leased assets. Let's dwell on this idea for a moment. If your organization were to create a new product or service, you would have the ability to develop a brand, a trademark or a patent because the organization owns the rights to that new product or service. With the advent of the knowledge age you are not able to trademark what your human capital assets dream. The human capital assets' minds are not the property of the organization. I agree that there may be an agreement in place that provides your organization with the results of the idea, but you still do not own the mind itself. You still do not own the concepts, ideas and potential solutions that the human capital assets develop. As an offshoot of the previous chapter, you do not own the results of the work of the empowered cross-functional team either.

The other aspect of Russ Moen's profile of the knowledge age human capital asset is that they are corporate leased assets. With unemployment levels where they are (according to national statistics, currently 3.6% in October 2019) the market is theoretically fully staffed. Indeed.com, at this time of writing, states that there are 39,000 available HR jobs in the country, and 978,000 management positions. Leave the human capital assets in a classical workplace and they can take their knowledge, skills and ideas and bring them elsewhere. They are leased assets because you only have them for as long as you meet their needs.

If we now lease their knowledge, how does that change their role in the TLS Continuum Empowerment Model? This new view of human capital assets has led to several major changes in your organization. First, with the advent of new knowledge, it has enabled the organization to dominate the product niche you are basing your business on. It has allowed you to be the first to market with new concepts, innovations and methods to resolve the customer's needs. The result is that the individual human capital assets are becoming empowered to deliver for the organization. Rather than being a number, the human capital assets are now valued and thus compensated based on their worth to the organization. This has come from a change in both the location and type of work being performed. It also means that there is no longer any type of censorship on what your human capital assets contribute. Consider for example what would have happened today, when the 3M employee suggested a new product we now know as Post-it Notes, was immediately censored because management did not like it.

Another change in the empowered organization is that management's view towards these new ideas plays out in the willingness to let human capital assets experiment with their ideas with the full understanding that if the experiment fails, that is okay. Management understands that failure is a natural part of experimentation.

I would argue that, with the evolution of the human capital asset role, they are now the primary cog in the model to empower your organization. They are the ones who better understand the nature of the organizational processes. As a human resource professional within your organization, it is your task to see that the organization moves towards this new direction. Human capital resources are vital to the successes of our businesses. You make the decision as to whether your organization maintains the status quo or heads in the direction of the new paradigm. This new paradigm calls for new strategies in order to maximize our human capital assets. This means we have to gain a better understanding of the importance of their roles. In my mind there are three key strategies that will carry us forward to the empowered organization. While these three strategies will be considered below on their own merits, simultaneously they are all interconnected. They are all part of the same organizational DNA we call empowerment. The three strategies consider engagement, ownership and subject matter expertise.

Strategy #1: Human Capital Assets Must Be Engaged in Their Work Environment on the Basis They Want (Engagement)

What does your workplace look like? More importantly, what does your workplace feel like? Is there an air of excitement? I would suggest to you that there are three types of human capital assets at play in your organization. The first are those that are not engaged in the organization in any form. They arrive in your workplace for the sole purpose to occupy time and space and get their paycheck. They are the ones who do as little as possible to say that they performed some work. They are actually, in the long run, costing you dollars. They are costing you dollars in rework. They are costing you in the failure to meet customer demands. They are costing you in the form of inefficient processes.

The second group is those who are slightly engaged. They are better than the totally unengaged, but are still not providing you with the resources to create that empowered organization.

The final group of human capital assets in your organization is totally engaged. This is the group upon which the empowered organization depends.

Depending on who you talk to, your organizations are faced, and in some ways blessed, with the presence of five generations in the workplace. While each and every one of them has the same ultimate goal—they want and seek a valued organization—the difference is that the road to that valued status differs from generation to generation. To create empowered individuals requires us to understand and take steps to meet their needs. These needs can be found in nine areas, as laid out in the works of David Stillman and Lynne Lancaster.[3] They state that generations are seeking ownership at work, flexibility in the workplace, a stable work environment, fair compensation, ability to advance their careers, respect from management and fellow employees, trust, adequate benefits and a safe work environment. The bottom line is that they are looking for a valued organization.

How do we recognize whether or not we are providing a valued organization to our human capital assets? There are two primary areas that contribute to this goal.

First, get rid of organizational silos. To play devil's advocate for a moment, some may make the argument that the parties to the silos are the experts on the issue. It is what they are being paid for. They understand the processes, solutions and the organization. As I showed in my earlier publication *Reality, Perception, and Your Company's Workplace Culture* (2019), this is not always the case.

Silos restrict thinking to a narrow range of views without the benefit of suggestions or solutions that are outside the bounds of the silo. The existence of silos limits the range of thought away from full spectrum thinking. Silos are a great way to show human capital assets that they are looking in a mirror and seeing nothing. If they are not part of the silo, the image they receive is that their thoughts and ideas are not worth anything. Silos tell your employees that they are not capable of understanding organizational problems. Silos perpetuate groupthink.

The solution is to open the lines of good communications. Open the channels so that your human capital assets are free to collaborate both internally and externally. Ensure that your actions demonstrate to your human capital assets that their ideas, suggestions and potential solutions are valued. Don't rule their ideas out out of hand as not working in your organization.

The second suggestion is to make the work environment a positive one. Consider alternative work methods that meet the need of your human capital assets. Open the work experience to increased flexitime opportunities. Open the work experience to, for example, Results Only Work Experience, as championed by Best Buy. Let the human capital assets dictate how they work, where they work and when they work as long, as the problem is solved, or the deadline is met.

The third suggestion is to ensure that the ultimate view of the organization is on the big picture. How do we resolve organizational issues? Be open to avenues for collaboration wherever the answers may come from. We enhance engagement when we entertain and permit full airing of all ideas regarding an issue. Some of these ideas may be contrary to what management thinks but we are not in a command and control mode here. The ideas must be given credibility. They must be given full airing. They must be played out to their conclusion, whether workable or not. At the same time, we must understand that just because a suggestion ends up not working in this situation, it may work at a later date.

Peter Pande in his book *The Six Sigma Way*, tells us that there is always a better way. Your human capital assets are constantly cognizant of ways to improve the system. Be open to these ideas. Do not immediately respond by saying "that is not the way we do things here." Do not immediately respond by saying "that won't work." You don't know the answer to that question if you have not tried it out in a simulation or a field trial. Your human capital assets are the ones who see the process in real time.

Here is a clue to engagement for you. When you construct an empowered cross-functional team, do they exceed their assignments and expectations? The empowered human capital asset, when they are engaged, will always do more than you think possible. The empowered human capital asset, when they are engaged, will always be willing to take risks in search of true solutions. The empowered human capital asset, when they are engaged, will always dream of solutions more than the classical organization thinks is practical. The empowered human capital asset, when they are engaged, will always expect more from your organization than you think possible. The empowered human capital asset, when they are engaged, will always care more for the value of their organization than the non-engaged individuals.

The sixth sign of the engaged human capital asset is that in the course of solving the problem at hand, if they do not have the skills or knowledge to complete a task, they will go out and develop the knowledge to complete the task. They care about their personal and professional development at all times. How does what I am doing now help me in the future to be a better person and a better employee? The path to resolve this question is to institute a dynamic coaching program to assist the employees to reach the level that is required.

Finally, you want a strong messenger for your organization. Get them involved and they will become that messenger. They will tell the world about their experiences. They will tell the world that they are valued by your organization. They will tell the world about the opportunities that exist in your organization. They become your primary talent acquisition tool.

Strategy #2: The Workplace Must Be Designed around a System That Provides the Avenue for the Employee to Enhance Their Learning of Skills That Will Improve the Way They Deliver What Is in Their Minds (Ownership)

A human capital asset is the single greatest part of your organizational DNA and thus of empowerment. In the empowered organization, the human capital assets are the crux to advancing innovation, process improvement and change management.

The demands of the VUCA world demand that human capital assets acquire the necessary skills and knowledge to better perform their responsibilities. Every time we encounter a change based on the volatility of the workplace; we are forced to do things differently. Every time we encounter a change that is derived from the uncertainty of the workplace, we need to prepare the organization for the next unexpected change. The goal is to reach a point where the human capital assets take responsibility for both the successes and failures of the organizational processes. When things go bad, they take the responsibility to make things right. When things go right, they champion that success to the organization and to the world. They take ownership of the process in order to ensure that there are more successes than failures. They understand under this ownership umbrella they have not only the ability but the right to stop the process in order to correct problems. They understand that in doing so there is no retaliation for making the decision. Management understands the reasons why they did what they did. Their fellow human capital assets understand the reasons why they did what they did.

Strategy #3: Whatever Processes We Put into Place Must Have As Their Goal the Manifestation That the Efforts Put Forth by the Human Capital Assets Are Appreciated by the Organization (Subject Matter Experts)

I asked earlier how you classify your human capital assets. The answer is really simple: They are the organizational subject matter experts for several reasons.

First, the human capital assets are the ones who understand the processes. Management sitting in the corner office or the professionals at lower level management may think they know the processes, but your frontline human capital assets are the real process experts. They are the ones who hear the voice of the customer in the form of the customer complaints. They are the ones who see when the production line is slowing down, so orders are late. They are the ones who see the end product and know whether it is meeting the specifications of the product order.

Encyclopedia.com[4] defines a subject matter expert as one with a high level of knowledge who performs specialized functions in organizational processes. It is important that we consider all functions in identifying our subject matter experts. It is also important that we include the subject matter experts on our empowered cross-functional teams.

In order for the human capital assets to become totally empowered, they must be provided with the opportunity to go and see the various steps to deliver the end product and/or service to the customer. This means that they should be given the opportunity to see the stages of the supply chain that comes before your organization gets involved. The purpose of these aspects is that the human capital assets gain knowledge of the processes that they might not already possess. This allows them to have a clear concept of the process involved.

The final aspect of the empowered individual process ownership may very well be the most important. W. Edwards Deming said it best when he said in his 14 Points of Quality that we need to drive out fear. The initial facet of this is to empower the human capital assets to take the chance on a solution. They need to be able to take the first three steps of the Design Thinking methodology. They have asked: What is the current situation? They have asked: What if they did this? The last of the three steps is to conduct experimentation in some form to determine if the solutions or hypotheses will work? The other side of the coin is that an empowered management will not hold any failures against the human capital assets. Management understands that each failure is actually a sign of how close we are getting to the correct solution.

As I stated at the start of the chapter, the empowered individual is the primary component of the TLS Continuum Empowerment Model. The individual human capital asset is the component that drives the processes within your organization. They are the ones who see the problems as they arise. They are the ones who can see the ways to correct the problems. The danger in not being an organization of empowered individuals is that nothing will get done in a manner which moves the organization forward.

Much of what I have discussed so far in this book can be considered to be mostly theoretical in nature. In the next chapter I want to apply this to the real world with real examples of the power of the model. I want to show you how the TLS Continuum Empowerment Model actually functions.

TLS Continuum Empowerment Model Goal Tree

In order to have

Total Empowerment and Engagement

I must have

Empowered Management

In order to have

Empowered Management

I must have

Set of Corporate Values
Established Corporate Goals
Established Corporate Strategies
Established Corporate Mission
Established Corporate Culture

In order to have

Empowered Teams

I must have

Diversity
Full Spectrum Thinking
Decision Tools
Established Cross-Functional Teams

In order to have

Empowered Individuals

I must have

Subject Matter Experts
Engagement
Process Ownership

Notes

1. Cadbury, Diane. *Chocolate Wars: The 150-Year Rivalry Between the World's Greatest Chocolate Makers.* New York, NY: Hachette Press, 2011.
2. Moen, Russ. *Love 'Em or Lose 'Em: Proven Strategies for Employee Retention.* Express Employment Professionals. January 21, 2009.
3. Lynne Lancaster and David Stillman are the co-authors of the books *When Generations Collide* and *The M-Factor.*
4. Encyclopedia.com. Definition of Subject Matter Expert. https://encyclopdeia.com/management/encyclopdeia-almanacs-transcriptsandmaps?subjectmatter experts

Chapter 8

Empowerment and Engagement

In Chapters 5, 6 and 7 I talked about the theory behind the TLS Continuum Empowerment Model. The presentation of a concept is fine, but for many of us we do not learn from a written presentation. Some of us have to hear it. Others have to be able to visualize the concept. The TLS Continuum Empowerment Model is just such a potential dilemma.

The TLS Continuum Empowerment Model is designed in such a manner as to provide you with a roadmap for how to change your organization from a classical organization into an empowered one. Figure 8.1 shows that in reality the three levels do not operate in a vacuum. They are all part of an interdependent system. They are all part of the HR system which supports your organization.

Chapter 8 will walk you through the implementation of that change, utilizing a real time example which utilizes an implementation process that is still ongoing. But before we look at that example let's review some preliminaries that we have touched on earlier in this book.

Dr. Lawrence Miller, a college classmate of mine at Parsons College in Iowa, wrote an article titled "Whole-System Architecture: A Model for Building the Lean Organization"[1]. In that article, Dr. Miller suggests that there are a few principles or paradigms of lean culture that will make a difference to how we build an empowered organization. The same concepts apply to the TLS Continuum Empowerment Model. Take a moment and consider how the following principles apply to your organization.

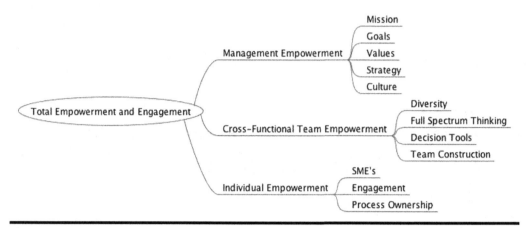

Figure 8.1   TLS Continuum Empowerment Model.

The World's Greatest Experts Have Their Hands on the Work

Your organization has engaged human capital assets because they own the organizational processes. Your organization has empowered human capital assets because they are engaged in the organizational processes. Our organizations depend on this essential relationship. Our organizations have both internal and external subject matter experts in order to achieve the level of innovation and change that the organization desires. The question then becomes: Who are the subject matter experts? Take a look in your organization for who you determine are the subject matter experts. I am willing to bet (and I am not a betting person) that your response will more often than not be the technical professionals within your organization. Problem on the production line? Talk to the engineers. Problem with a bill? Ask the finance professionals. Miller points out that the world's greatest subject matter experts have their hands on the work to be performed. This message changes or should change your answer.

If Miller is correct, then who really are the subject matter experts? The greatest experts in any organization are those who are on the front line in the process. They operate and observe the processes of the workplace. They are the ones who hear the customer complain. They are the ones who can tell you when something is not right. They can even tell you what the cause of the problem is. Toyota has included an Anton option allowing any assembly line worker to stop a process when there is a problem. This does not mean that you can't disagree with their conclusions; it just establishes that the ones with the best answers are those who are the ones with firsthand knowledge of the process. As the subject matter experts, their views need to be given genuine consideration. In *Reality and Perception and Your Company's Workplace Culture: Creating the New Normal for Problem Solving and Change Management*, I conducted two plant simulation tours, and in both cases, it was not the technical professional who pointed out the problems but the shipping clerk who explained the start of the process. In Bob Sproull's goal tree simulation, it was the junior accountant who filled a gap in the process.

In order to reach the status of an empowered organization we need to have each and every one within the organization on the same page. We need to have each and every one within the organization involved as a subject matter expert in their respective area of responsibility, with an overview of how that responsibility fits into the broader organizational view.

Continuously Improve, Every Day

Workplace conditions of today most likely will not be the conditions of tomorrow. The ever-presenence of the impact of VUCA on the workplace changes our lives on a daily basis. We work in a volatile workplace. We work in an uncertain workplace. We work in a chaotic workplace. Things change in the flash of an eye. This means whatever life brings us, we must be able to react in response. The direct result is that we need to look to make changes to our processes each and every day in order to achieve the strategic alignment we are striving for. Peter Pande, in his book *The Six Sigma Way*, tells us that there is always a better way. Part of the empowerment effort has to be the recognition that the VUCA world is going to demand that we look for ways to improve the system every time we begin a process. Earlier in this book I discussed the formula shown below.

$$CPI = MS \times EMP \times ENG \times TMG$$

Continuous Process Improvement consists of four components. The first is the management style of the organization. Management needs to eliminate the command and control mentality from their thinking and operating thoughts. In the TLS Continuum Empowerment Model, the emphasis must be on providing the base structure of the organization. Management is also responsible for the organization's values, its mission, its culture, its goals and its strategies, along with the tenets of the alignment with the organization's persona in the workplace. Management's role is to coach the organization on how to reach that alignment in a fashion which improves the organization and brings about innovation.

The second factor in the continuous process improvement is empowerment within the organization. In the empowered organization, the organization finds its power in the value and contribution of its human capital assets. They come to work ready to work, not just to collect a paycheck. These efforts are seen from the perspective of the individual but also from the wider view of the corporation in the global workplace. Empowerment means that we no longer are involved in the blame-game. If there is a problem, we collectively seek a solution, we do not begin by saying it is someone else's problem. Empowerment means that the human capital assets take ownership not just of their own contributions but the contributions of the organization as a whole. My contention is that if we ensure that the three levels of the model are engaged then this factor will self-identify itself. If the teams and individuals function at a higher level, at the ownership level, empowerment will take care of itself.

The third factor is that of engagement. Engagement is a key word in the global workplace. The Gallup Organization measures engagement level in the workplace and it becomes a valuable measure of how well your organization is doing. Forbes Magazine[2] states that employee engagement is the level of commitment, passion and loyalty a worker has towards their work and company. The more engaged an employee is, the more work they'll put forth.

It tells us whether the human capital assets are working not only for the benefit of the organization but for their own self-improvement. The organization is moving towards an environment where the value of the human capital assets is not only recognized but appreciated. Where the organization does not separate contribution and reward levels based on where they are in the company. Where the organization understands the value and importance of the human capital assets using whatever tools they need to resolve an issue. This is true whether the source for the solution is internal to the organization or external, whether the source for the solution is in a relationship with the organization or not. Work is done in a result-only work environment. The importance of the engagement effort is that the human capital assets understand that they are a real part of the organization. The migration away from a just a number who does not show up in the mirror changes to a view of significant importance and contribution to the workplace.

Work Flows Horizontally, Not Vertically

Empowerment is only going to occur when we understand and accept that work does not flow from the corner office to the factory floor. Empowerment is only going to occur when we understand and accept that work does not flow from the production line to the customer. The organizational work moves across the supply chain.

I looked at this earlier when I discussed the SIPOC form. Consider this in more detail. Your customer receives their order based on the processes. The supply chain commences when the first part of the finished product is created, and it flows along the course of the chain from one link to another until it reaches the final end user. Let me suggest another example. Whenever we produce a process map or a value stream map it is always depicted in a horizontal fashion. We are always depicting things as a sequence of events. It begins at a starting point and finishes at an end point. The steps are laid out as a chain in horizontal presentation.

We Win As Teams

The final segment of the Continuous Process Improvement formula is that of teamwork. The nature of your organizational teamwork is your prerogative. Peter Scholtes in his book *The Team Handbook, 3rd edition* suggests that you can have temporary project teams. You can have ongoing or functional work teams which are longstanding teams. Finally, you can have technologically based virtual teams. In each case you are given the opportunity to operate the teams under a classic mode or an empowered mode. You can operate under the classical team and allow the results of the team efforts to be guided by groupthink and narrowly focused or you can operate under the empowered team and open the solution process to a wider view of the solution possibilities. This is how we get things done within the organization.

The teams that can perform like the GE Workout or the GE CAP program are the ones who achieve their goals through empowerment. In 1960, a University of Massachusetts trained chemical engineer named Jack Welch joined a company called General Electric. In 1971 he was chosen to be the 8th President and Chairman of the Board of the organization. From our research, he understood that our organizations were overburdened by bureaucracy and non-value-added parts of the process that had nothing to do with customer needs. As a result, Jack Welch pushed the operating companies to find ways to improve how they did things.

From the very beginning of his tenure within C-Suite, he took every opportunity to find ways to clean up, if you will, the structure of the organization through careful analysis of the individual processes from the perspective of effectiveness and efficiency.

One tool that came out of this new focus of the organization was the implementation of the GE Workout around 1989. The GE Workout consisted of a very structured system to resolve problems within the organization. The continuous process improvement developed along the paths shown in Figure 8.2.

Welch was firmly against the overbearing bureaucracy found within the GE organization. What he did believe in was the ability of every employee, no matter his or her role within the organization, to have a say in its future. The basic premise of the GE workout was that cross-functional teams would identify a problem and create solutions to solve that problem. This process of cross-functional teams being the conduit for change within the organization was the impetus for the Workout program.

The GE Workout consisted of a five-step process as we describe below:

Step 1: Problem Identification – In the process of delivering the services needed to meet the customer's needs, employees determine that there is a problem with the process which prohibits the organization

Figure 8.2   GE Workout.

from meeting the customer's deadline. As a result, a collaborative effort is made to identify exactly what the process roadblock is and its impact on the organization.

Step 2: Team Development – Following the identification of the problem a team was put in place which consisted of both rank and file and management to apply a review process to the indicated problem. The team makeup consisted of both internal and external stakeholders. The key to to the inclusion of a particular team member was what the impact of that team member from the problem to the solution.

Step 3: Town Meeting – Once the solutions to the identified problems were designed the team brought the discussion of the problem to a town meeting where both the teams and the members of upper management were present. These town meetings could, according to David Ulrich's book on the workout process, last from one to three days. Each team presented their findings and recommendations to the management team. The report presentations also included the justification behind the solutions.

Step 4: Upper Management Decision – At the conclusion of each team presentation, upper management was provided with two alternatives. The first is that they could reject the project completely, the second alternative was that management could provide the green light to complete the project.

Step 5: Sponsorship – If upper management gave its approval to go forward with the problem resolution, one of the team members steps forward and assumes the role of the project sponsor to guide the project going forward. It is their responsibility to ensure that the solutions are implemented within 90 days typically. It involved frequent progress reports back to the organizational management.

As the years passed a group from GE management began to look at how we could improve the workout process. Understand it was not that anyone disapproved of the workout process, it was just this inbred part of the GE culture that you constantly looked at how to improve the process to make it more robust. The result was what GE called the Change Acceleration Process or CAP.

The CAP pilot was run out of the GE training center at Crotonville, New York, which was originally termed the Leadership Development Series. At the same time Larry Bossidy, who later went on to write the book *Execution*, developed another program with similar elements and goals.

The two were combined to form the CAP. It consisted of a model which contained six steps which were reviewed on the basis of where we are today, where we are going to end up and how to make the transition. The process began with the requirement of management to lead the change effort. Management had to buy into the change in order for it to function successfully.

Following management leading the change process, the CAP established the reason why the organization had to share the need across the entire organization. They demonstrated why the change that was introduced needed to cross the entire organization, not departmental silos alone. They demonstrated to the rank and file how this change was going to make their job easier and better. Keep in mind our ultimate goal is to produce our services or projects cheaper, better and faster. The rank and file needed to understand what it was that was in the process for them.

Having proven the need to solve the problem, management turned to creating a vision for the organization. This vision provided a roadmap, much as we are doing with establishing our road to HR excellence. As can be seen by the descriptions of the GE workout and the CAP, the empowered teams have the power to make suggestions for process improvement and then implement them without management diktats (command and control); they are the ones who will bring about innovation and improvement.

As I stated earlier, the best way to understand the working of an empowered team is to see one in action. I could not conceive a better example of this than to look at the March for Our Lives movement. This is not a forum to debate the goal they had set. That is better designed for a different forum then this book. I highly suggest that you take the time to really read the books *#Never Again* by David and Lauren Hogg and *We say #Never Again: Reporting by the Parkland Student Journalists* as edited by Melissa Falkowki and Eric Garner. They are highly emotionally charged and deserve the time to understand and comprehend their experience.

Case Study: Marjory Stoneman Douglas High School[3]: The TLS Continuum Empowerment Model in Real Time

Valentine's Day 14 February 2018 began as a typical late winter day in Florida. Temperatures were in the low 80s. The 2,800 students arrived for the start of classes bringing baked goods and valentines for fellow students and their other halves. The day progressed like any normal school day, until about 2pm when a former student entered the school and proceeded to gun down 17 of their fellow students, before being apprehended by local law enforcement. This was the catalyst for an empowered team that changed their lives. This was the catalyst for empowered individuals that changed their lives. This case study describes how their efforts utilized the TLS Continuum Empowerment Model to carry on after the tragedy.

Timeline

February 14, 2018	School shooting at Marjory Stoneman Douglas HS
February 14, 2018	Phone call from Producer at CNN
February 21, 2018	Student March on Tallahassee
February 21, 2018	White House meeting with President Trump
February 21, 2018	CNN Town Hall in Parkland, Florida
March 14, 2018	Nationwide Student Walkout
March 24, 2018	March for Our Lives march in Washington and Internationally
April 20, 2018	Nationwide Student Walkout

Empowered Management

The first level of the Empowerment Model is represented by the empowered manager. In this case study that group is represented by two different aspects. The first is the school administration which has put in place an environment where the students are placed in a nurturing space. The second is the faculty advisors who serve not as command and control managers, but as coaching managers. This is what Melissa Falkowski and Eric Garner, who are teachers at the Marjory Stoneman Douglas High School serving as the journalism teacher and the broadcasting teacher respectively, did with the students following the mass shooting at the school. In each case they were there in a support role. Their focus was to assist the students in dealing with their feelings about the events of the day.

They established goals for the students going forward, which was the completion of the two remaining projects for the year. The first was the next edition of the school newspaper, *Eagle's Eye*, titled "In Memoriam", in which they had to prepare the obituaries of each of the 17 individuals killed in the shooting. The two advisors supported the students in writing the content, considering many of those killed were close friends or relatives. The students were encouraged to recognize their feelings as well as pay proper respect to the victims of the massacre. The end result had at least a two-page spread for each victim with pictures along with a description of who they were in the words of students (see: https://issuu.com/melissafalkowski4/docs/memorial_donate). Under normal conditions, writing obituaries can be difficult but with their personal involvement it became even more difficult.

The second project was the newspaper's final edition for the year, which was titled "Take a Stand", which began the effort to create the March for Our Lives movement. In the issue the students talked about the steps required to bring about the changes they were seeking, including their manifesto (see: https://issuu.com/melissafalkowski4/docs/4thquarterfull). As can be seen in the above timeline, the events following the shooting came fast and furious keeping everyone in fast mode to achieve their goals and strategies.

Empowered Cross-Functional Team

One of the ways that the students dealt with their grief was to create a response to that grief in the form of a movement to change the policies of this country. The movement was totally student led and done with a small group of 20 students who had the skills to deal with the media environment so as to get their message out. Each of the students was involved within the classes that Melissa Falkowski and Eric Garner taught or the extra-curricular programs that they advised.

The cross-functional team began by finding their cause, which was the push for gun control law changes. Their cause was essentially chosen for them due to the aftermath of the shooting. The second stage was controlling their message. The team was very careful of how the message was placed in today's multi-outlet world. A lot of their message was conducted through social media. One of the other lessons the students learned was to stay within their roots. The movement, they understood, was inherent on them holding on to the core of the group. Those 20 students became the face of the effort.

The next step in the process was to mobilize their social media contacts nationwide to begin to build the movement the team had established. The key was to keep the population engaged and involved in the action being undertaken.

I talked earlier about diversity of ideas and part of the team's efforts was centered on others becoming part of the leadership, to open the discussions to full spectrum thinking.

Empowered Individual

Part of the curriculum at Marjory Stoneman Douglas High School is that the teachers encourage the students to express their ideas and thoughts in their writings. By conducting their research for their articles, they became the subject matter experts on the issue that was confronting them. Because they felt that the issue was close to home, they were more engaged in the process because they owned the outcomes.

Results

The results of the efforts of the original group are that the March for Our Lives movement now stretches beyond Parkland, Florida. The organization has expanded beyond the initial 20 students to regional and international offices with individuals carrying the message forward.

The TLS Continuum Empowerment Model is a new perspective on organizational change management. It calls for an expanded involvement of the human capital assets. I began with the argument that in life, DNA is the necessary fact for our existence. In the workplace, empowerment is that DNA which will sustain change management.

Empowerment will not happen without the engagement and ownership of the organizational processes. Engagement comes from the recognition that our human capital assets have real value to the success of the organization. That value comes from going beyond a number system for them. It goes beyond having human capital assets filling time and space.

It is our hope that this presentation of the model will at least get you to think differently about the way you consider change management in your organization. It is our belief that if you expand the diversity of thought and avenues for process ownership you will in turn expand engagement and will fortify empowerment in your organization. The model will fortify your relationships with the stakeholders both internally and externally.

Notes

1. Miller, Lawrence. "Whole-System Architecture: A Model for Building the Lean Organization" www.lmmiller.com/wp-content/uploads/2011/06/Whole-System-Architecture-Article1.pdf
2. Forbes.com. "How to Establish a Culture of Employee Engagement" www.forbes.com/sites/mikekappel/2018/01/04/how-to-establish-a-culture-of-employee-engagement/#3e93b0378dc4
3. Based on the book *We Say #Never Again*, a collection of reporting by the Parkland Student Journalists. New York, NY: Crown Publishers, 2019.

Acknowledgments

Employee Empowerment: The Prime Component of Sustainable Change Management represents my sixth publishing endeavor. It is a continuing part of my journey to show the workplace the benefits of change management to their organizations. There is an old adage which says practice makes perfect. However, writing a book does not necessarily become easier or more perfect each and every time.

Writing a book takes a community to produce the finished product. We are deeply appreciative of those members of my professional network who have helped us along the way. I am especially appreciative of Bob Sproull who is a certified Jonah from the Goldratt Institute and has been willing to provide his thoughts and explanations when I got stuck on a concept.

During my Six Sigma Black Belt training, I learned my lessons well and have with some effort found the path to relate them to the business arena. Despite learning those lessons, it was still critical that my efforts be reviewed by independent eyes with the mission to determine whether we got the material across in a manner easily understood by the everyday business professional. For their willingness to review the final work, I thank Bill Mazurek who was my black belt instructor and has become a friend and colleague. I have to extend an added thank you to Melissa Falkowski, who not only was helpful with the case study but lived through the events of 14 February 2018.

I would like to thank my college classmate Dr. David Cohen for his willingness to take time out of his busy schedule to write the Foreword for this book. His insight to organizational behavior is critical for my understanding of change management.

I am also appreciative of the vast network of contacts that I have established over the past decade who have been a great asset. In particular I am thankful to Steven Browne, Mike Wilkerson, and Bob Sproull who have graciously written endorsements for this current work.

This work would not have come to fruition if it were not for the assistance of the staff at Productivity Press including Michael Sinocchi our editor, Iris Fahrer our Project Editor and Kathryn Kadian, Michael's editorial assistant. Thank you for your time and efforts to bring this message to the business world.

Further Reading

Articles

Heathfield, Susan. "Top 10 Principles of Employee Empowerment." https://www.the-balancecareers.com/top-principles-of-employee-empowerment-1958658

Huis, Marloes. "A Three-Dimensional Model of Women's Empowerment Implications in the Field of Microfinance and Future Directions." https://nebi.nim.nih.gov/p.me/articles/pmc5625516

Kanter, Rosabeth. "Kanter's Theory of Structural Empowerment." https://structura-lempowerment.weebly.com/kanters-theory.html

Limeade Marketing. "The Importance of Employee Empowerment in the Workplace." https://www.Limeade.com/2018/04/importance-of-employee-empowerment-in-the-workplace

Lotch, Patricia. "13 Characteristics of an Employee Empowered Culture." https://the-thrivingsmallbusiness.com/empowerment-a leadership-competency

Yip, Kam-Shing. "The Empowerment Model: A Critical Reflection of Empowerment in Chinese Culture." https://academic.oup.com/article-abstract/49/3/479/194079?redirectedFrom=pdf

Cox, James and John G. Schleier

Theory of Constraints Handbook. New York, NY: McGraw Hill, 2010. Chapter 26 is totally devoted to education.

Liker, Jeffrey et al.

The Toyota Way: 14 Management Principles from the World's Greatest Manufacturer. New York, NY: McGraw-Hill, 2003.

The Toyota Way Fieldbook. New York, NY: McGraw-Hill, 2005.

Toyota Talent: Developing Your People the Toyota Way. New York, NY: McGraw-Hill, 2007.

Toyota Culture: The Heart and Soul of the Toyota Way. New York, NY: McGraw-Hill, 2008.

Toyota Way to Lean Leadership: Achieving and Sustaining Excellence through Leadership Development. New York, NY: McGraw-Hill, 2011a.

The Toyota Way to Continuous Improvement: Linking Strategy and Operational Excellence to Achieve Superior Performance. New York, NY: McGraw-Hill, 2011b.

Sproull, Bob et al.

The Ultimate Improvement Cycle: Maximizing Profits through the Integration of Lean, Six Sigma and the Theory of Constraints. New York, NY: CRC Press, 2009.

Epiphanized: Integrating Theory of Constraints, Lean and Six Sigma. Great Barrington, MA: North River Press, 2012.

Index

Printed in the United States
By Bookmasters